Software Engineering 2004

Curriculum Guidelines for Undergraduate
Degree Programs in Software Engineering

A Volume of the Computing Curricula Series

23 August 2004

The Joint Task Force on Computing Curricula
IEEE Computer Society
Association for Computing Machinery

This material is based upon work partially supported by the
National Science Foundation under Grant No. 0003263

IEEE Computer Society Order Number C2350
ISBN-13: 978-0-7695-2350-7
ISBN-10: 0-7695-2350-1
Library of Congress Number 2006921876
ACM Order Number 999061

Additional copies may be ordered from:

IEEE Computer Society	IEEE Service Center	IEEE Computer Society	ACM Order Department
Customer Service Center	445 Hoes Lane	Asia/Pacific Office	P.O. Box 11405
10662 Los Vaqueros Circle	P.O. Box 1331	Watanabe Bldg., 1-4-2	New York, NY 10286-1405
P.O. Box 3014	Piscataway, NJ 08855-1331	Minami-Aoyama	1-800-342-6626
Los Alamitos, CA 90720-1314	Tel: + 1 732 981 0060	Minato-ku, Tokyo 107-0062	1-212-626-0500 (outside U.S.)
Tel: + 1 800 272 6657	Fax: + 1 732 981 9667	JAPAN	orders@acm.org
Fax: + 1 714 821 4641	http://shop.ieee.org/store/	Tel: + 81 3 3408 3118	
http://computer.org/cspress	customer-service@ieee.org	Fax: + 81 3 3408 3553	
csbooks@computer.org		tokyo.ofc@computer.org	

Individual paper REPRINTS may be ordered at: reprints@computer.org

Cover art production by Joseph Daigle/Studio Productions

Printed in the United States of America

This material is based upon work partially supported by the
National Science Foundation under Grant No. 0003263

Preface

This document was developed through an effort originally commissioned by the ACM Education Board and the IEEE Computer Society Educational Activities Board to create curriculum recommendations in several computing disciplines: computer science, computer engineering, software engineering, and information systems. Other professional societies have joined in a number of the individual projects. Such has notably been the case for the Software Engineering 2004 (SE2004) project, which has included representatives from the Australian Computer Society, the British Computer Society, and the Information Processing Society of Japan.

Development process

The SE2004 project has been driven by a steering committee appointed by the sponsoring societies. The development process began with the appointment of the steering committee cochairs and several other participants in the fall of 2001. More committee members, including representatives from the other societies were added in the first half of 2002. The following are the members of the SE2004 Steering Committee:

Cochairs
> Rich LeBlanc, ACM, Georgia Institute of Technology, US
> Ann Sobel, IEEE-CS, Miami University, US

Knowledge area chair
> Ann Sobel, Miami University, US

Pedagogy focus group cochairs
> Mordechai Ben-Menachem, Ben-Gurion University, Israel
> Timothy C. Lethbridge, University of Ottawa, Canada

Co-editors
> Jorge L. Díaz-Herrera, Rochester Institute of Technology, US
> Thomas B. Hilburn, Embry-Riddle Aeronautical University, US

Organizational representatives
> ACM: Andrew McGettrick, University of Strathclyde, UK
> ACM SIGSOFT: Joanne M. Atlee, University of Waterloo, Canada
> ACM Two-Year College Education: Elizabeth K. Hawthorne, Union County College, US
> Australian Computer Society: John Leaney, University of Technology Sydney, Australia
> British Computer Society: David Budgen, Keele University, UK
> Information Processing Society of Japan: Yoshihiro Matsumoto, Musashi Institute of Technology, Japan
> IEEE-CS Technical Committee on Software Engineering: J. Barrie Thompson, University of Sunderland, UK

Acknowledgments

The National Science Foundation, the Association of Computing Machinery, and the IEEE Computer Society have supported the development of this document.

Since its inception, many individuals have contributed to the SE2004 project, some in more than one capacity. This work could not have been completed without the dedication and expertise of these volunteers. Appendix B lists the names of those who have participated in the various development and review stages of this document. Special thanks go to Susan Mengel of Texas Tech University who served as an original cochair of the steering committee and performed the initial organizational tasks for the SE2004 project.

Table of Contents

Preface.. iii

Acknowledgments.. iv

Chapter 1.   Introduction 1

    1.1   Purpose of this volume 1
    1.2   Where we fit in the Computing Curriculum picture 1
    1.3   Development process of the SE2004 volume 2
        1.3.1   Education Knowledge Area group 2
        1.3.2   Pedagogy Focus Area group.. 3
        1.3.3   Full volume development 3
    1.4   Structure of the volume 3

Chapter 2.   The Software Engineering Discipline 5

    2.1   The discipline of software engineering... 5
    2.2   Software engineering as a computing discipline... 6
    2.3   Software engineering as an engineering discipline... 7
        2.3.1   Characteristics of engineering 7
        2.3.2   Engineering design 8
        2.3.3   Domain-specific software engineering 8
    2.4   Professional Practice 9
        2.4.1   Rationale.. 9
        2.4.2   Software Engineering Code of Ethics and Professional Practices 9
        2.4.3   Curriculum support for professional practice... 10
    2.5   Prior software engineering education and computing curriculum efforts................... 10
    2.6   SWEBOK and other BOK efforts 11

Chapter 3:   Guiding Principles.. 13

    3.1   SE2004 principles 13
    3.2   Student outcomes 14

Chapter 4:   Overview of Software Engineering Education Knowledge 17

    4.1   Process of determining the SEEK.. 17
    4.2   Knowledge areas, units, and topics... 17
    4.3   Core material.. 18
    4.4   Unit of time 18
    4.5   Relationship of the SEEK to the curriculum... 19
    4.6   Selection of knowledge areas.. 19
    4.7   SE education knowledge areas... 20
    4.8   Computing essentials 21
    4.9   Mathematical and engineering fundamentals.. 23
    4.10   Professional practice.. 24
    4.11   Software modeling and analysis 25
    4.12   Software design.. 27
    4.13   Software verification and validation.. 28

4.14   Software evolution 29

4.15   Software process 30

4.16   Software quality 31

4.17   Software management 32

4.18   Systems and application specialties 33

Chapter 5:   Guidelines for SE Curriculum Design and Delivery 36

5.1   Guideline regarding those developing and teaching the curriculum 36

5.2   Guidelines for constructing the curriculum 37

5.3   Attributes and attitudes that should pervade the curriculum and its delivery 39

5.4   General strategies for software engineering pedagogy 44

5.5   Concluding comment 46

Chapter 6:   Courses and Course Sequences 47

6.1   Course coding scheme 48

6.2   Introductory sequences covering software engineering, computer science, and mathematics material 49

   6.2.1   Introductory computing sequence A: Start software engineering in first year 51

   6.2.2   Introductory computing sequence B: Introduction to software engineering in second year 52

   6.2.3   Introductory mathematics sequences 53

6.3   Core software engineering sequences 54

   6.3.1   Core software engineering package I 55

   6.3.2   Core software engineering package II 56

   6.3.3   Software engineering capstone project 57

6.4   Completing the curriculum: Additional courses 57

   6.4.1   Courses covering the remaining compulsory material 57

   6.4.2   Non-SEEK courses 58

6.5   Curriculum patterns 59

Chapter 7:   Adaptation to Alternative Environments 66

7.1   Alternative teaching environments 66

   7.1.1   Students at different physical locations 67

   7.1.2   Students in class at different times 67

7.2   Curricula for alternative institutional environments 68

   7.2.1   Articulation problems 68

   7.2.2   Coordination with other university curricula 68

   7.2.3   Cooperation with other institutions 69

7.3   Programs for associate-degree-granting institutions in the United States and community colleges in Canada 70

   7.3.1   Special programs 71

Chapter 8:   Program Implementation and Assessment 72

8.1   Curriculum resources and infrastructure 72

   8.1.1   Faculty 72

   8.1.2   Students 72

   8.1.3   Infrastructure 72

   8.1.4   Industry participation 73

8.2   Assessment and accreditation issues 73

8.3   SE in other computing-related disciplines 74

Bibliography for Software Engineering Education 76

Appendix A: Detailed Descriptions of Proposed Courses 84

Appendix B: Contributors and Reviewers 119

Index 128

Notes

Chapter 1: Introduction

1.1 Purpose of this volume

This volume's primary purpose is to provide guidance to academic institutions and accreditation agencies about what should constitute an undergraduate software engineering education. These recommendations have been developed by a broad, internationally based group of volunteer participants. This group has taken into account much of the work that has been done in software engineering education over the last quarter of a century. Software engineering curriculum recommendations are of particular relevance, as there is currently a surge in new software engineering degree programs, and accreditation processes for such programs have been established in a number of countries.

The recommendations in this volume are based on a high-level set of characteristics of software engineering graduates, which is presented in chapter 3. Flowing from these outcomes are the document's two main contributions:

- Software Engineering Education Knowledge (SEEK): what every SE graduate must know

- Curriculum: ways to teach this knowledge and the skills fundamental to software engineering various contexts

1.2 Where we fit in the Computing Curriculum picture

In 1998, the Association for Computing Machinery (ACM) and the Computer Society of the Institute for Electrical and Electronic Engineers (IEEE-CS) convened a joint-curriculum task force called *Computing Curricula 2001,* or *CC2001* for short. In its original charge, the CC2001 Task Force was asked to develop a set of curricular guidelines that would "match the latest developments of computing technologies in the past decade and endure through the next decade." This task force came to recognize early in the process that they—as a group primarily composed of computer scientists—were ill-equipped to produce guidelines that would cover computing technologies in their entirety. Over the last 50 years, *computing* has become an extremely broad designation that extends well beyond the boundaries of computer science to encompass such independent disciplines as computer engineering, software engineering, information systems, and many others. Given that domain's breadth, the curriculum task force concluded that no group representing a single specialty could hope to do justice to computing as a whole. At the same time, feedback they received on their initial draft made it clear that the computing education community strongly favored a report that took into account the discipline's breadth.

The task force's solution to this challenge was to continue the development of a volume of computer science curriculum recommendations, published in 2001 as the *CC2001 Computer Science* volume (CCCS volume) [IEEE 2001b]. In addition, they recommended to their sponsoring organizations that the project be broadened to include volumes of recommendations for the related disciplines listed above, as well as any others that might be deemed appropriate by the computing education community. This volume represents the work of the Software

Engineering 2004 (SE2004) project and is the first such effort by the ACM and the IEEE-CS to develop curriculum guidelines for software engineering.

In late 2002, *IS 2002—Model Curriculum and Guidelines for Undergraduate Degree Programs in Information Systems* was approved and published, having been created by a task force chartered by the ACM, the IEEE-CS, the Association for Information Systems (AIS), and the Association of Information Technology Professionals (AITP). Additional efforts are ongoing to produce recommended curricula for computer engineering and information technology.

1.3   Development process of the SE2004 volume

The construction of this volume has centered around three major efforts that have engaged numerous volunteers, as well as all of the Steering Committee members. The first of these efforts was the development of a set of desired curriculum outcomes and a statement of what every SE graduate should know. The second effort involved determining and specifying the knowledge to be included in an undergraduate software engineering program, the Software Engineering Education Knowledge (SEEK). The third effort was the construction of a set of curriculum recommendations that described how a software engineering curriculum, incorporating the SEEK, could be structured in various contexts.

1.3.1   Education Knowledge Area group

Work began on the volume in earnest in the spring of 2002 with the assignment of Education Knowledge Area volunteers to develop an initial body of SEEK. The volunteers were given an initial set of education knowledge areas, each with a short description, and were charged with defining the units and topics for each knowledge area using the templates developed by the steering committee. In addition, the results of activities undertaken at an open workshop held at the Conference on Software Engineering Education & Training (CSEE&T 2002) [Thompson 2002], and of discussions about required curriculum knowledge content, held at the Summit on Software Engineering Education in conjunction with the International Conference of Software Engineering (ICSE 2002) [Thompson 2004], provided input to the SEEK developers.

The volunteers' initial work was incorporated into a preliminary draft of the SEEK, which was the working document used in an NSF-sponsored workshop on the SEEK, held in June 2002. This workshop brought together Education Knowledge Area group members, steering committee members, leaders in software engineering education, and selected Pedagogy Focus Area group members to work on the preliminary draft. The steering committee subsequently refined the workshop artifacts.

A set of internationally recognized software engineering experts performed a selected review of the resulting SEEK document. The steering committee used their evaluations and comments to produce the first official draft version of the SEEK, which was released for public review in August 2002.

When the first review window terminated in early October 2002, the steering committee had received approximately 40 reviews. Each evaluation was coupled with a written response from the steering committee including committee action and justification. After posting the second version of the SEEK in December 2002, another round of reviews were solicited until the beginning of March 2003. The Working Group on Software Engineering Education and Training (WGSEET) were instrumental in sharpening the content of this version to best match the Pedagogy Focus Area group's curriculum guidelines. The WGSEET's contributions along with the second set of evaluations has brought the SEEK to its final version.

1.3.2 Pedagogy Focus Area group

In October 2002, the Pedagogy Focus Area group began work on producing the curriculum recommendations using the SEEK as a foundation. The group formed a Pedagogy Focus Area group process and work plan. Group members began work on defining the pedagogy guidelines, curriculum models, international adaptation, and implementation environments. The steering committee refined this information in February 2003. Reviews of this draft of the Pedagogy Chapter occurred during a meeting of the WGSEET and at a workshop held at the 2003 Conference on Software Engineering Education and Training in March.

The preliminary draft of the Pedagogy Chapter contained the following sections:
- Principles of Software Engineering Curriculum Design and Delivery
- Proposed curricula, including curriculum models and sample courses outlining the topics of the SEEK covered in a particular course
- International adaptation
- Classes of skills and problems that students should master, in addition to learning the knowledge in the SEEK
- Adaptation to alternative educational environments, such as two-year colleges

The curriculum models presented were developed using the SEEK, the Computer Science volume (CCCS), and a survey of existing bachelor degree programs. A total of 32 programs from North America, Europe, and Australia were identified and characterized to aid in this work. A key technique to developing the models rested on identifying which SEEK topics would be covered by reusing existing CCCS courses. The remaining SEEK material was distributed into software engineering courses, using the existing programs as a guide.

1.3.3 Full volume development

In the spring and summer of 2003, additional material (introduction, guidelines and outcomes, software engineering background, and so on) was included with the SEEK and the curriculum components to construct a full draft of the SE2004 volume. The first review of the draft SE2004 volume was carried out at the Second Summit on Software Engineering Education held at ICSE 2003 [Thompson 2003]. The steering committee used input from the summit and other informal reviews to produce the first public draft of the full SE2004 volume, which was submitted for review from July 2003 to September of 2003. The ACM Education Board and the IEEE-CS Educational Activities Board also reviewed and commented on the draft. Reviewer comments and further work by the steering committee resulted in the current final version of the SE2004 volume.

1.4   Structure of the volume

Chapter 2 discusses the nature of software engineering as a discipline, describing some of the history of software engineering education, and explaining how these elements have influenced this document's recommendations. Chapter 3 presents the guiding principles behind the document's development. These principles were adapted from those originally articulated by the CC2001 Task Force as they began work on what became the CCCS volume. Chapter 3 also provides the description of what every SE graduate should know. Chapter 4 presents the body of the SEEK, which underlies the curriculum guidelines and educational program designs presented in chapters 5 and 6, respectively. Chapter 7 discusses adapting the curriculum recommendations in chapter 6 to alternative environments. Finally, chapter 8 addresses various curriculum implementation challenges and also considers assessment approaches.

Chapter 2:   The Software Engineering Discipline

This chapter discusses the nature of software engineering and some of the history and background that is relevant to the development of software engineering curriculum guidance. The purpose of the chapter is to provide context and rationale for the curriculum materials in subsequent chapters.

2.1   The discipline of software engineering

Since the dawn of computing in the 1940s, the applications and uses of computers have grown at a staggering rate. Software plays a central role in almost all aspects of daily life: government, banking and finance, education, transportation, entertainment, medicine, agriculture, and law. The number, size, and application domains of computer programs have grown dramatically, and, as a result, hundreds of billions are being spent on software development. Most people's lives and livelihoods depend on this development's effectiveness. Software products help us be more efficient and productive. They make us more effective problem solvers, and they provide us with an environment for work and play that is often safer, more flexible, and less confining.

Despite these successes, there are serious problems in the cost, timeliness, and quality of many software products. Many reasons for these problems exist, including:

- Software products are among the most complex man-made systems, and software by its very nature has intrinsic, essential properties (for example, complexity, invisibility, and changeability) that are not easily addressed [Brooks 95].

- Programming techniques and processes that are effective when used by an individual or small team to develop modest-sized programs do not scale well to the development of large, complex systems (that is, systems with millions of lines of code requiring years of work by hundreds of software developers).

- The pace of change in computer and software technology drives the demand for new and evolved software products. This situation has created customer expectations and competitive forces that strain our ability to produce quality software within acceptable development schedules.

It has been more than 35 years since the first organized, formal discussion of software engineering as a discipline took place at the 1968 NATO Conference on Software Engineering [Naur 1969]. The term "software engineering" is now widely used in industry, government, and academia; hundreds of thousands of computing professionals go by the title "software engineer"; numerous publications, groups and organizations, and professional conferences use software engineering in their names; and many educational courses and programs on software engineering exist. However, disagreements and differences of opinion about the meaning of the term remain. The following definitions provide several views of the meaning and nature of software engineering. Nevertheless, they all possess a common thread, which states (or strongly implies) that software engineering is more than just coding; it includes quality, schedule, economics, and the knowledge and application of principles and discipline.

Definitions of software engineering

Over the years, numerous definitions of the discipline of software engineering have been presented. For the purpose of this document, we highlight the following definitions:

- "The establishment and use of sound engineering principles (methods) in order to obtain economically software that is reliable and works on real machines" [Bauer 1972].

- "Software engineering is that form of engineering that applies the principles of computer science and mathematics to achieving cost-effective solutions to software problems" [CMU/SEI-90-TR-003].

- "The application of a systematic, disciplined, quantifiable approach to the development, operation, and maintenance of software" [IEEE 1990].

Aspects of each of these definitions contribute to the perspective of software engineering used in the construction of this volume. One particularly important aspect is that software engineering builds on computer science and mathematics. But, in the engineering tradition, it goes beyond this technical basis to draw on a broader range of disciplines.

These definitions clearly state that software engineering is about creating high-quality software in a systematic, controlled, and efficient manner. Consequently, there are important emphases on analysis and evaluation, specification, design, and evolution of software. In addition, issues related to management and quality, novelty and creativity, standards, individual skills, and teamwork and professional practice play a vital role in software engineering.

2.2   Software engineering as a computing discipline

A common misconception about software engineering is that it is primarily about process-oriented activities (that is, requirements, design, quality assurance, process improvement, and project management). In this view, competency in software engineering can be achieved by acquiring a strong engineering background, a familiarity with a software development process, and a minimal computing background, including experience using one or more programming languages. Such a background is, in fact, quite insufficient. The misconception that leads to such thinking is based on an incomplete view of the nature and challenges of software engineering.

In the historical development of computing, computer scientists produced software and electrical engineers produced the hardware on which the software ran. As software's size, complexity, and critical importance grew, so did the need to ensure that it performed as intended. By the early 1970s, it was apparent that proper software development practices required more than just the underlying principles of computer science; they need both the analytical and descriptive tools developed within computer science and the rigor that the engineering disciplines bring to the reliability and trustworthiness of the artifacts they engineer.

Software engineering is thus different in character from other engineering disciplines, due to both the intangible nature of software and the discrete nature of software operation. Software engineering seeks to integrate the principles of mathematics and computer science with the engineering practices developed to produce tangible, physical artifacts. Drawing on computing and mathematics as foundations, software engineering seeks to develop systematic models and reliable techniques for producing high-quality software. These concerns extend all the way from theory and principles to the development practices that are most visible to those outside the discipline. Although it is unlikely that every software engineer will have deep expertise in all aspects of computing, a general understanding of the aspects' relevance and some expertise in particular aspects are necessary. The definition of the body of SEEK described in chapter 4 reflects the reliance of software engineering on computer science, with the largest SEEK component being computing essentials.

2.3　Software engineering as an engineering discipline

The study and practice of software engineering is influenced both by its roots in computer science and its emergence as an engineering discipline. A significant amount of current software engineering research is conducted within the context of computer science and computing departments or colleges. Similarly, software engineering degree programs are being developed by such academic units as well as engineering colleges. Thus, the discipline of software engineering can be seen as an engineering field with a stronger connection to its underlying computer science discipline than the more traditional engineering fields. In the process of constructing this volume, particular attention has been paid to incorporating engineering practices into software development, so as to distinguish this curriculum from computer science curricula. To prepare for the more detailed development of these ideas, this section examines the engineering methodology and how it applies to software development.

We must also point out that although strong similarities exist between software engineering and more traditional engineering (as listed in section 2.3.1), there are also some differences (not necessarily to the detriment of software engineering):

- Foundations are primarily in computer science, not natural sciences.

- The focus is on discrete rather than continuous mathematics.

- The concentration is on abstract/logical entities instead of concrete/physical artifacts.

- There is no "manufacturing" phase in the traditional sense.

- Software "maintenance" primarily refers to continued development, or evolution, and not to conventional wear and tear.

2.3.1　Characteristics of engineering

There is a set of characteristics that is not only common to every engineering discipline, but is so predominant and critical that it can be used to describe the underpinnings of engineering. These underpinnings should be viewed as desirable characteristics of software engineers. Thus, they have influenced both the development of software engineering and the content of this volume.

[1] Engineers proceed by making a series of decisions, carefully evaluating options, and choosing an approach at each decision-point that is appropriate for the current task in the current context. Appropriateness can be judged by tradeoff analysis, which balances costs against benefits.

[2] Engineers measure things, and when appropriate, work quantitatively. They calibrate and validate their measurements, and they use approximations based on experience and

empirical data.

[3] Engineers emphasize the use of a disciplined process when creating a design and can operate effectively as part of a team in doing so.

[4] Engineers can have multiple roles: research, development, design, production, testing, construction, operations, and management in addition to sales, consulting, and teaching.

[5] Engineers use tools to apply processes systematically. Therefore, the choice and use of appropriate tools is key to engineering.

[6] Engineers, via their professional societies, advance by the development and validation of principles, standards, and best practices.

[7] Engineers reuse designs and design artifacts.

Although the following sections use the terms "engineer" and "engineering" extensively, this document is about the design, development, and implementation of undergraduate software engineering curricula. It must be acknowledged that much of the work in this document is based on the work of numerous individuals and groups that have advanced the state of computer science and information technology, and have developed programs that help prepare graduates to practice software development in a professional manner.

2.3.2 Engineering design

Design is central to any engineering activity and it plays a critical role in software. In general, engineering design activities refer to the definition of a new artifact by finding technical solutions to specific practical issues, while accounting for economic, legal, and social considerations. As such, engineering design provides the prerequisites for the physical realization of a solution by following a systematic process that best satisfies a set of requirements within potentially conflicting constraints.

Software engineering differs from traditional engineering because of the special nature of software, which places a greater emphasis on abstraction, modeling, information organization and representation, and the management of change. Software engineering also includes implementation and quality-control activities normally considered part of the manufacturing process of the product cycle. Furthermore, continued evolution (that is, maintenance) is also more critical for software. Even with this broader scope, however, a central challenge of software engineering is still the kind of decision-making known as engineering design. An important aspect of this challenge is the need to apply the supporting process at multiple levels of abstraction. An increasing emphasis on reuse and component-based development holds hope for new, improved practices in this area.

2.3.3 Domain-specific software engineering

Within a domain, an engineer relies on specific education and experience to evaluate possible solutions, keeping in mind various factors related to function, cost, performance, and manufacturability. Engineers must determine which standard parts can be used and which parts must be developed from scratch. To make the necessary decisions, they must have a fundamental knowledge of the domain and related specialty subjects.

Domain-specific techniques, tools, and components typically provide the most compelling software engineering success stories. Great leverage has been achieved in well-understood domains in which standard implementation approaches have been widely adopted. To prepare themselves for professional practice, graduates of software engineering programs should come to terms with the fundamentals of at least one application domain. That is, they should understand the problem space that defines the domain as well as common approaches, including standard components (if any), used in producing software to solve problems in that domain.

2.4   Professional practice

A key objective of any engineering program is to provide graduates with the tools necessary to begin the professional practice of engineering. As chapter 3 indicates, an important guiding principle for this document is, "The education of all software engineering students must include student experiences with the professional practice of software engineering." Subsequent chapters discuss the content and nature of such experiences, while this section provides rationale and background for the inclusion of professional practice elements in a software engineering curriculum.

2.4.1   Rationale

Professionals have special obligations requiring them to apply specialist knowledge on behalf of members of society who do not have such knowledge. All of the characteristics of engineering discussed in section 2.3.1 relate, directly or indirectly, to the professional practice of engineering. Employers of graduates from engineering programs often speak to these same needs [Denning 1992]. Each year, the National Association of Colleges and Employers conducts a survey to determine what qualities employers consider most important in applicants seeking employment [NACE 2003]. In 2003, employers were asked to rate the importance of candidate qualities and skills on a five-point scale, with five being "extremely important," and one being "not important." Communication skills (4.7), honesty/integrity (4.7), teamwork skills (4.6), interpersonal skills (4.5), motivation and initiative (4.5), and strong work ethic (4.5) were the most desired characteristics.

The dual challenges of society's critical dependence on the quality and cost of software and the relative immaturity of software engineering make attention to professional practice issues even more important to software engineering programs than to many other engineering programs. Graduates of software engineering programs need to arrive in the workplace equipped to meet these challenges and to help evolve the software engineering discipline into a more professional and accepted state. Like other engineering professionals, when appropriate and feasible, software engineers should seek quantitative data on which to base decisions, yet should also be able to function effectively in an environment of ambiguity and avoid the limitations of oversimplified or unverified formula-based modeling.

2.4.2   Software Engineering Code of Ethics and Professional Practices

Software engineering as a profession has obligations to society. The products produced by software engineers affect the lives and livelihoods of the clients and users of those products.

Hence, software engineers need to act in an ethical and professional manner. The preamble to the *Software Engineering Code of Ethics and Professional Practice* [ACM 1998] states:

> "Because of their roles in developing software systems, software engineers have significant opportunities to do good or cause harm, to enable others to do good or cause harm, or to influence others to do good or cause harm. To ensure, as much as possible, that their efforts will be used for good, software engineers must commit themselves to making software engineering a beneficial and respected profession. In accordance with that commitment, software engineers shall adhere to the following Code of Ethics and Professional Practice."

To help ensure ethical and professional behavior, software engineering educators have an obligation to not only make their students familiar with the Code, but also find ways for students to engage in discussion and activities that illustrate and illuminate the Code's eight principles, including common dilemmas facing professional engineers in typical employment situations.

2.4.3   Curriculum support for professional practice

A curriculum can have an important direct effect on some professional practice factors (such as teamwork, communication, and analytic skills), while others (such as strong work ethic and self-confidence) are subject to the more subtle influence of a college education on an individual's character, personality, and maturity. In this volume, chapter 4 identifies elements of professional practice that should be part of any curriculum and expected student outcomes. Chapters 5 and 6 contain guidance and ideas for incorporating material about professional practice into a software engineering curriculum. In particular, the chapters include material directly supportive of professional practice, such as technical communications, ethics, and engineering economics, and ideas about modeling work environments, such as case studies, laboratory work, and team project courses.

Many elements, some outside the classroom, can significantly affect a student's preparation for professional practice. Examples include involvement in the core curriculum by faculty with professional experience, student work experience as an intern or in a cooperative education program, and extracurricular activities, such as attending colloquia, field trips visits to industry, and participation in student professional clubs and activities.

2.5   Prior software engineering education and computing curriculum efforts

In the late 1970s, the IEEE-CS initiated an effort to develop curriculum recommendations for software engineering, which were used in the creation of a number of master's programs across the United States [Freeman 1976, Freeman 1978]. Although this effort centered on graduate education, it formed the basis for a focus on software engineering education in general. The first undergraduate-level software engineering programs in the UK commenced at Imperial College in 1985 and at the University of Sheffield in 1988 [Finkelstein 1993, Cowling 1998].

In the late 1980s and early 1990s, efforts of the Education Group of the Software Engineering Institute (SEI) at Carnegie Mellon University fostered and supported software engineering education. These efforts included surveying and reporting on the state of software engineering education, publishing curriculum recommendations for graduate software engineering programs, instituting a master's of software engineering program at CMU, organizing and facilitating workshops for software engineering educators, and publishing software education curriculum modules [Budgen 2003, Tomayko 1999].

The SEI initiated and sponsored the first Conference on Software Engineering Education and Training in 1987. The CSEET has since provided a forum for SE educators to meet, present, and discuss SE education issues, methods, and activities. In 1995, as part of its education program, the SEI started the WGSEET (http://www.sei.cmu.edu/collaborating/ed/workgroup-ed.html). The WGSEET objective is to investigate issues, propose solutions and actions, and share information and best practices with the software engineering education and training community. In 1999, the working group produced a technical report offering guidelines on the design and implementation of undergraduate software engineering programs [Bagert 1999]. Outside the US, several national and international efforts have sought to raise awareness of issues related to software engineering education. Most of these efforts have consisted of education streams within larger events (for example in the 1996 Professional Awareness in Software Engineering Conference [Myers, 1997]), or small conferences devoted to software engineering education, such as the IFIP 1993 Working Conference in Hong Kong [Barta, 1993] and an international symposium held in Rovaniemi, Finland, in 1997 [Taipale, 1997]).

In 1993, the IEEE-CS and the ACM established the IEEE-CS/ACM Joint Steering Committee for the Establishment of Software Engineering as a Profession. Subsequently, the steering committee was replaced by the Software Engineering Coordinating Committee (SWECC), which coordinated the work of three efforts: the development of a Code of Ethics and Professional Practices [ACM 1998]; the Software Engineering Education Project (SWEEP), which developed a draft accreditation criteria for undergraduate programs in software engineering [Barnes 1998]; and the development of the *Guide to the Software Engineering Body of Knowledge* (SWEBOK) [Bourque 2001]. The Curriculum 1991 report [Tucker 1991] and the CCCS volume [IEEE 2001b] have also influenced the structure and content of this document. All of these efforts have influenced the volume's philosophy and content.

2.6   SWEBOK and other BOK efforts

A major challenge in providing curriculum guidance for new and emerging, or dynamic, disciplines is the identification and specification of the discipline's underlying content. Because the computing disciplines are both relatively new and dynamic, specification of a body of knowledge is critical.

Chapter 4 specifies a body of knowledge that supports software engineering education curricula (SEEK). The organization and content was influenced by several previous efforts to describe the knowledge that comes from other related disciplines. The following is a description of such efforts:

- The SWEBOK is a comprehensive description of the knowledge needed for the practice of software engineering. One of the project's objectives was to "provide a foundation for curriculum development." To support this objective, the SWEBOK includes a rating system for its knowledge topics based on Bloom's levels of educational objectives [Bloom 1956]. Although the SWEBOK was one of the primary sources used in the SEEK's development, and there has been close communication between the SWEBOK and SE2004 projects, some assumptions and features of the SWEBOK differentiate the two efforts:

> The SWEBOK is intended to cover knowledge after four years of practice.

> The SWEBOK intentionally does not cover non-software engineering knowledge that a software engineer must have.

> The SE2004 is intended to support only undergraduate software engineering education.

- The PMBOK (*Guide to the Project Management Body of Knowledge*) [PMI 2000] describes knowledge about project management (not limited to software projects). In addition to its relevance to software project management, the PMBOK's organization and style has influenced similar efforts in the computing disciplines.

- The IS 97 report (*Model Curriculum and Guidelines for Undergraduate Degree Programs in Information Systems*) [Davis, 1997] describes a model curriculum for undergraduate degree programs in information systems. The document describes an IS body of knowledge, which includes SE knowledge, and also includes a metric similar to Bloom's levels for prescribing the required depth of knowledge for undergraduates.

- The "Computing as a Discipline" report [ACM 1989] provides a comprehensive definition of computing and formed the basis for the work on Computing Curriculum 1991 and its successor Computing Curriculum 2001. It specifies nine subject areas that cover the computing discipline, including software engineering.

- The *Guidelines for Software Engineering Education* [Bagert 1999] (developed by the WGSEET) describes a curriculum model for undergraduate software engineering education that is based on a body of knowledge consisting of four areas: foundations, core, recurring, and support.

Chapter 3:   Guiding Principles

This chapter describes the foundational ideas and beliefs that guided the development of the SE2004 materials: the guiding principles for the entire SE2004 effort and the desired student outcomes for an undergraduate curriculum in software engineering.

3.1   SE2004 principles

The following list of principles was strongly influenced by the CCCS principles, and in some cases represents minor rewording of those principles. In other cases, we have tried to capture the special nature of software engineering that differentiates it from other computing disciplines.

[1] *Computing is a broad field that extends well beyond the boundaries of any one computing discipline.* SE2004 concentrates on the knowledge and pedagogy associated with a software engineering curriculum. Where appropriate, it will share or overlap material contained in other Computing Curriculum reports and will offer guidance on its incorporation into other disciplines.

[2] *Software engineering draws its foundations from a wide variety of disciplines.* Undergraduate study of software engineering relies on many areas in computer science for its theoretical and conceptual foundations, but it also requires students to use concepts from various other fields, such as mathematics, engineering, and project management, and one or more application domains. All software engineering students must learn to integrate theory and practice, recognize the importance of abstraction and modeling, be able to acquire special domain knowledge beyond the computing discipline for the purposes of supporting software development in specific application domains, and appreciate the value of good design.

[3] *The rapid evolution and the professional nature of software engineering require an ongoing review of the corresponding curriculum.* The professional associations in this discipline must establish an ongoing review process that allows individual components of the curriculum recommendations to be updated on a recurring basis. Also, because software engineers have special professional responsibilities to the public, the curriculum guidance should support and promote effective external assessment and accreditation of software engineering programs.

[4] *Development of a software engineering curriculum must be sensitive to changes in technologies, practices, and applications, new developments in pedagogy, and the importance of lifelong learning.* In a field that evolves as rapidly as software engineering, educational institutions must adopt explicit strategies for responding to change. Institutions, for example, must recognize the importance of remaining abreast of well-established progress in both technology and pedagogy, subject to the constraints of available resources. Software engineering education, moreover, must seek to prepare students for lifelong learning that will enable them to move beyond today's technology to meet the challenges of the future.

[5] *SE2004 must go beyond knowledge elements to offer significant guidance in terms of individual curriculum components.* The SE2004 curriculum models should assemble the knowledge elements into reasonable, easily implemented learning units. Articulating a set of

well-defined curriculum models will make it easier for institutions to share pedagogical strategies and tools. It will also provide a framework for publishers who provide the textbooks and other materials.

[6] *SE2004 must support the identification of the fundamental skills and knowledge that all software engineering graduates must possess.* Where appropriate, SE2004 must help define the common themes of the software engineering discipline and ensure that all undergraduate program recommendations include this material.

[7] *Guidance on software engineering curricula must be based on an appropriate definition of software engineering knowledge.* The description of this knowledge should be concise, appropriate for undergraduate education, and should use the work of previous studies on the software engineering body of knowledge. From this description, a core set of required topics must be specified for all undergraduate software engineering degrees. The core should have broad acceptance by the software engineering education community. Coverage of the core will start with the introductory courses, extend throughout the curriculum, and be supplemented by additional courses that can vary by institution, degree program, or individual student.

[8] *SE2004 must strive to be international in scope.* Although curricular requirements differ from country to country, SE2004 must be useful to computing educators throughout the world. Where appropriate, every effort should be made to ensure that the curriculum recommendations are sensitive to national and cultural differences so that they will be widely applicable throughout the world. The involvement of national computing societies and volunteers from all countries should be actively sought and welcomed.

[9] *The development of SE2004 must be broadly based.* To be successful, the process of creating software engineering education recommendations must include participation from the many perspectives represented by software engineering educators and by industry, commerce, and government professionals.

[10] *SE2004 must include exposure to aspects of professional practice as an integral component of the undergraduate curriculum.* The professional practice of software engineering encompasses a wide range of issues and activities, including problem solving, management, ethical and legal concerns, written and oral communication, working as part of a team, and remaining current in a rapidly changing discipline.

[11] *SE2004 must include discussions of strategies and tactics for implementation, along with high-level recommendations.* Although it is important for SE2004 to articulate a broad vision of software engineering education, the success of any curriculum depends heavily on implementation details. SE2004 must provide institutions with advice on the practical concerns of setting up a curriculum.

3.2   Student outcomes

As a first step in providing curriculum guidance, the following set of outcomes for an undergraduate curriculum was developed. This is intended as a generic list that is adaptable to a variety of software engineering program implementations.

Graduates of an undergraduate SE program must be able to

[1] *Show mastery of the software engineering knowledge and skills and the professional issues necessary to begin practice as a software engineer.*

Students, through regular reinforcement and practice, need to gain confidence in their abilities as they progress through a software engineering program of study. In most instances, students acquire knowledge, as well as skills, through a staged approach in which they achieve different levels as each academic term progresses. In addition, graduates must have an understanding and appreciation of professional issues related to ethics and professional conduct, economics, and societal needs.

[2] *Work both individually and as part of a team to develop and deliver quality software artifacts.*

Students need to complete tasks that involve work as an individual but also many other tasks that entail working with a group. For group work, students should be informed of the nature of groups and group activities and roles as explicitly as possible. This must include an emphasis on the importance of such matters as a disciplined approach, adhering to deadlines, communication, and individual as well as team performance evaluations.

[3] *Reconcile conflicting project objectives, finding acceptable compromises within limitations of cost, time, knowledge, existing systems, and organizations.*

Students should engage in exercises that expose them to conflicting, and even changing, requirements. There should be a strong real-world element present in such cases to ensure that the experience is realistic. Curriculum units should address these issues with the aim of ensuring high quality requirements and a feasible software design.

[4] *Design appropriate solutions in one or more application domains using software engineering approaches that integrate ethical, social, legal, and economic concerns.*

Throughout their study, students should be exposed to a variety of appropriate approaches to engineering design in the general sense, and to specific problem solving in various applications domains for software. They need to be able to understand the strengths and the weaknesses of the available options and the implications of selecting the appropriate approach for a given situation. Their proposed design solutions must be made within the context of ethical, social, legal, security, and economic concerns.

[5] *Demonstrate an understanding of and apply current theories, models, and techniques that provide a basis for problem identification and analysis, software design, development, implementation, verification, and documentation.*

The Capstone project, an important activity at the end of a software engineering program of study, offers students the opportunity to tackle a major project and demonstrate their ability to bring together topics from a variety of courses and apply them effectively. This requirement should also include the ability to reflect on their achievements.

[6] *Demonstrate an understanding and appreciation of the importance of negotiation, effective work habits, leadership, and good communication with stakeholders in a typical software development environment.*

A program of study should include at least one major activity that involves producing a solution for a client. Software engineers must take the view that they have to produce software that is of genuine utility. Where possible, we should integrate within the program a period of industrial experience, as well as invited lectures from practicing software engineers, and even involvement in such activities as external software competitions. All of this provides a richer experience and helps create an environment that supports production of high-quality software engineering graduates.

[7] *Learn new models, techniques, and technologies as they emerge and appreciate the necessity of such continuing professional development.*

By the end of their program of study, students should show evidence of being self-motivated lifelong learners. Such a situation is achieved through a series of stages inserted throughout a program of study. In later academic years, such as at the capstone stage, students should be ready and willing to learn new ideas. But again, students need to be exposed to best practices in earlier stages.

Chapter 4:   Overview of Software Engineering Education Knowledge

This chapter describes the body of knowledge that is appropriate for an undergraduate program in software engineering. The knowledge is designated as the SEEK (Software Engineering Education Knowledge).

4.1   Process for determining the SEEK

The development model chosen for determining SE2004 was based on the model used to construct the CCCS volume. The initial selection of the SEEK areas was based on the SWEBOK knowledge areas and multiple discussions with dozens of SEEK area volunteers. The SEEK area volunteers were divided into groups representing individual SEEK areas, with each group containing roughly seven volunteers. These groups were assigned the task of providing the details of the units composing a particular educational knowledge area and further refining these units into topics. To facilitate their work, references to existing related software engineering body of knowledge efforts (SWEBOK, CSDP Exam, and SEI curriculum recommendations, for example) and a set of templates for supporting the generation of units and topics were provided.

After the volunteer groups generated initial drafts of details about their individual education knowledge areas, the Steering Committee held a face-to-face forum that brought together education knowledge and pedagogy area volunteers to iterate the individual drafts and generate an initial draft of the SEEK (see Appendix B for an attendee list). This workshop, with this particular goal, mirrored a similar overwhelmingly successful workshop held by CCCS at the same point in their development process. Once the education knowledge area content was stabilized, topics were identified as core or elective. Topics were also labeled with one of three of Bloom's taxonomy levels of educational objectives: knowledge, comprehension, or application. Only these three levels of learning were chosen because they represent the knowledge that can be reasonably learned during an undergraduate education.

After the workshop, a draft of the SEEK was completed. Subsequently, the SEEK draft went through an intensive internal review (by a group of selected software engineering experts) and several widely publicized public reviews. After each review was completed, the Steering Committee used the reviewer comments to further refine and improve the content of the SEEK.

4.2   Knowledge areas, units, and topics

The term "knowledge" is used to describe the whole spectrum of content for the discipline: information, terminology, artifacts, data, roles, methods, models, procedures, techniques, practices, processes, and literature. The SEEK is organized hierarchically into three levels. The highest level is the education **knowledge area**, which represents a particular subdiscipline of software engineering that is generally recognized as a significant part of the body of software engineering knowledge that an undergraduate should know. Knowledge areas are high-level structural elements used for organizing, classifying, and describing software engineering knowledge. Each area is identified by an abbreviation, such as PRF for professional practices.

Each knowledge area is broken down into smaller divisions called **units,** which represent individual thematic modules within an area. Adding a two- or three-letter suffix to the area identifies each unit—for example, PRF.com is a unit on communication skills.

Each unit is further divided into a set of **topics,** which is the lowest level of the hierarchy.

4.3   Core material

In determining the SEEK, it is recognized that software engineering, as a discipline, is relatively young and that common agreement on the definition of an education body of knowledge is evolving. The SEEK developed and presented in this document is based on a variety of previous studies and commentaries on the recommended content for the discipline. It was specially designed to support the development of undergraduate software engineering curricula, and therefore does not include all of the knowledge that would exist in a more generalized body of knowledge representation. Hence, a body of **core** knowledge has been defined. The core consists of the essential material that professionals teaching software engineering agree is necessary for anyone attempting to obtain an undergraduate degree in this field. By insisting on a broad consensus in defining the core, it is hoped that the core will be as small as possible, giving institutions the freedom to tailor the curriculum's elective components to meet their individual needs.

The following points should be emphasized to clarify the relationship between the SEEK and the steering committee's ultimate goal of providing undergraduate software engineering curriculum recommendations.

- *The core is not a complete curriculum.* Because the core is defined as minimal, it does not by itself constitute a complete undergraduate curriculum. Every undergraduate program will include additional units, both within and outside the software engineering body of knowledge, which this document does not attempt address.

- *Core units are not necessarily limited to a set of introductory courses taken early in the undergraduate curriculum.* Although many of the units defined as core are indeed introductory, some core units must clearly be covered only after students have developed significant background in the field. For example, topics in such areas as project management, requirements elicitation, and abstract high-level modeling might require knowledge and sophistication that lower-division students do not possess. Similarly, introductory courses can include elective units[1] alongside the coverage of core material. The designation *core* simply means *required* and says nothing about the level of the course in which it appears.

4.4   Unit of time

The SEEK must define a metric that establishes a standard of measurement with which to judge the actual amount of time required to cover a particular unit. Choosing such a metric was quite difficult because no standard measure is recognized throughout the world. For consistency with the earlier curriculum reports, namely the other computing curricula volumes related to this

---

[1] Material offered as part of an undergraduate program that falls outside the core is considered to be *elective*.

effort, it was decided to express time in **hours**. An hour corresponds to the actual in-class time required to present the material in a traditional lecture-oriented format (referred to in this document as contact hours). To dispel any potential confusion, however, it is important to underscore the following observations about the use of lecture hours as a measure:

- *The steering committee does not seek to endorse the lecture format.* Even though we have used a metric that has its roots in a classical, lecture-oriented format, the steering committee believes that there are other styles—particularly given recent improvements in educational technology—that can be at least as effective. For some of these styles, the notion of hours might be difficult to apply. Even so, the time specifications should at least serve as a comparative measure, in the sense that a five-hour unit will presumably take roughly five times as much time to cover as a one-hour unit, independent of the teaching style.

- *The hours specified do not include time spent outside of class.* The time assigned to a unit does not include the instructor's preparation time or the time students spend outside of class. As a general guideline, the amount of out-of-class work is approximately three times the in-class hours (three hours in class and nine outside).

- *The hours listed for a unit represent a minimum level of coverage.* The time measurements assigned for each unit should be interpreted as the *minimum* amount of time necessary for a student to perform the unit's learning objectives. It is always appropriate to spend more time on a unit than the mandated minimum.

4.5   Relationship of the SEEK to the curriculum

The SEEK does not represent the curriculum, but rather provides the foundation for the design, implementation, and delivery of the educational units that make up a software engineering curriculum. Other chapters of the SE2004 volume provide guidance and support on how to use the SEEK to develop a curriculum. In particular, the organization and content of the knowledge areas and knowledge units should not be deemed as implying how the knowledge should be organized into education units or activities. For example, the SEEK does not advocate a sequential ordering of the KAs (1st CMP, 2nd FND, 3rd PRF, and so on). Nor does it suggest how topics and units should be combined into education units. Furthermore, the SEEK is not intended to purport any special curriculum development methodology (waterfall, incremental, cyclic, and so on).

4.6   Selection of knowledge areas

The SWEBOK Guide provided the starting point for determining knowledge areas. Because both the SE2004 Steering Committee and the SEEK area volunteers felt strongly about emphasizing the academic discipline of software engineering, the area chosen to represent the theoretical and scientific foundations of developing software products eventually grew to one half the size of the core. This prompted a reevaluation of whether the original goal of emphasizing the discipline was indeed being met. The resulting set of knowledge areas was rebalanced to support these goals. The result stresses the fundamental principles, knowledge, and practices underlying the software engineering discipline in a form suitable for undergraduate education.

4.7   SE education knowledge areas

Ten knowledge areas make up the SEEK: Computing Essentials (CMP), Mathematical & Engineering Fundamentals (FND), Professional Practice (PRF), Software Modeling & Analysis (MAA), Software Design (DES), Software Verification & Validation (VAV), Software Evolution (EVL), Software Process (PRO), Software Quality (QUA), and Software Management (MGT). The knowledge areas do not include material about continuous mathematics or the natural sciences; other parts of the SE2004 volume will discuss the needs in these areas. For each knowledge area, there is a short description and then a table that delineates the units and topics for that area. Recommended contact hours are designated for each knowledge unit. A Bloom's taxonomy level (indicating the capability a graduate should possess) and the topic's relevance (indicating whether the topics is essential, desirable, or optional to the core) are designated for each topic. Table 1 summarizes the SEEK knowledge areas, with their sets of knowledge units, and lists the minimum number of hours recommended for each area and unit.

Bloom's attributes are specified using the letters k, c, or a, which represent

- Knowledge (k): remembering previously learned material. Test observation and recall of information—that is, "bring to mind the appropriate information" (such as dates, events, places, knowledge of major ideas, and mastery of subject matter).

- Comprehension (c): understanding information and the meaning of material presented. For example, a graduate should be able to translate knowledge to a new context, interpret facts, compare, contrast, order, group, infer causes, and predict consequences.

- Application (a): ability to use learned material in new and concrete situations. For example, the graduate should use information, methods, concepts, and theories to solve problems requiring the skills or knowledge presented.

A topic's relevance to the core is represented as follows:

- Essential (E): The topic is part of the core.

- Desirable (D): The topic is not part of the core, but it should be included in particular program's core if possible; otherwise, it should be considered elective materials.

- Optional (O): The topic should be considered as elective only.

KA/KU	Title	hrs	KA/KU	Title	hrs
CMP	**Computing Essentials**	**172**	**VAV**	**Software V & V**	**42**
CMP.cf	Computer science foundations	140	VAV.fnd	V&V terminology and foundations	5
CMP.ct	Construction technologies	20	VAV.rev	Reviews	6
CMP.tl	Construction tools	4	VAV.tst	Testing	21
CMP.fm	Formal construction methods	8	VAV.hct	Human computer UI testing and evaluation	6
			VAV.par	Problem analysis and reporting	4
FND	**Mathematical & Engineering Fundamentals**	**89**	**EVL**	**Software Evolution**	**10**
FND.mf	Mathematical foundations	56	EVO.pro	Evolution processes	6
FND.ef	Engineering foundations for software	23	EVO.ac	Evolution activities	4
FND.ec	Engineering economics for software	10			
PRF	**Professional Practice**	**35**	**PRO**	**Software Process**	**13**
PRF.psy	Group dynamics/psychology	5	PRO.con	Process concepts	3
PRF.com	Communications skills (specific to SE)	10	PRO.imp	Process implementation	10
PRF.pr	Professionalism	20			
MAA	**Software Modeling & Analysis**	**53**	**QUA**	**Software Quality**	**16**
MAA.md	Modeling foundations	19	QUA.cc	Software quality concepts and culture	2
MAA.tm	Types of models	12	QUA.std	Software quality standards	2
MAA.af	Analysis fundamentals	6	QUA.pro	Software quality processes	4
MAA.rfd	Requirements fundamentals	3	QUA.pca	Process assurance	4
MAA.er	Eliciting requirements	4	QUA.pda	Product assurance	4
MAA.rsd	Requirements specification & documentation	6			
MAA.rv	Requirements validation	3			
DES	**Software Design**	**45**	**MGT**	**Software Management**	**19**
DES.con	Design concepts	3	MGT.con	Management concepts	2
DES.str	Design strategies	6	MGT.pp	Project planning	6
DES.ar	Architectural design	9	MGT.per	Project personnel and organization	2
DES.hci	Human–computer interface design	12	MGT.ctl	Project control	4
DES.dd	Detailed design	12	MGT.cm	Software configuration management	5
DES.ste	Design support tools and evaluation	3			

* Section 4.18 (Systems and application specialties) includes additional material, which is not part of the core, that can be used to extend core knowledge and provide for specialization.

4.8   Computing essentials

Description

Computing essentials include the computer science foundations that support the design and construction of software products. This area also includes knowledge about the transformation of a design into an implementation, the tools used during this process, and formal software construction methods.

Units and Topics

Reference		k,c,a	E,D,O	Hours	Related Topics
CMP	**Computing Essentials**			172	
CMP.cf	*Computer science foundations*			140	
CMP.cf.1	Programming fundamentals (CCCS PF1 to PF5) (control and data, typing, recursion)	a	E		
CMP.cf.2	Algorithms, data structures/representation (static and dynamic), and complexity (CCCS AL 1 to AL 5)	a	E		CMP.ct.1,CMP.fm.5,MAA.cc.1

CMP.cf.3	Problem-solving techniques	a	E	CMP.cf.1
CMP.cf.4	Abstraction—use and support for (encapsulation, hierarchy, and so on)	a	E	MAA.md.1
CMP.cf.5	Computer organization (CCCS, parts AR 1 to AR 5)	c	E	
CMP.cf.6	Basic concept of a system	c	E	MAA.rfd.7
CMP.cf.7	Basic user human factors (I/O, error messages, robustness)	c	E	DES.hci
CMP.cf.8	Basic developer human factors (comments, structure, readability)	c	E	CMP.cf.1
CMP.cf.9	Programming language basics (key concepts from CCCS PL1-PL6)	a	E	CMP.ct.3,CMP.ct.4
CMP.cf.10	Operating system basics (key concepts from CCCS OS1-OS5)	c	E	CMP.ct.10,CMP.ct.15
CMP.cf.11	Database basics	c	E	DES.con.2
CMP.cf.12	Network communication basics	c	E	
CMP.cf.13	Semantics of programming languages		D	
CMP.ct	*Construction technologies*			20
CMP.ct.1	API design and use	a	E	DES.dd.4
CMP.ct.2	Code reuse and libraries	a	E	CMP.cf.1
CMP.ct.3	Object-oriented run-time issues (for example, polymorphism and dynamic binding)	a	E	CMP.cf.1,9,DES.str.2
CMP.ct.4	Parameterization and generics	a	E	CMP.cf.1
CMP.ct.5	Assertions, design by contract, defensive programming	a	E	MAA.md.2
CMP.ct.6	Error handling, exception handling, and fault tolerance	a	E	DES.con.2,VAV.tst.2,VAV.tst.9
CMP.ct.7	State-based and table-driven construction techniques	c	E	FND.mf.7,MAA.tm.2,CMP.cf.10
CMP.ct.8	Run-time configuration and internationalization	a	E	DES.hci.6
CMP.ct.9	Grammar-based input processing (parsing)	a	E	FND.mf.8
CMP.ct.10	Concurrency primitives (such as semaphores and monitors)	a	E	CMP.cf.10
CMP.ct.11	Middleware (components and containers)	c	E	DES.dd.3,5
CMP.ct.12	Construction methods for distributed software	a	E	CMP.cf.2
CMP.ct.13	Constructing heterogeneous (hardware and software) systems; hardware-software codesign	c	E	DES.ar.3
CMP.ct.14	Performance analysis and tuning	k	E	FND.ef.4,DES.con.6,CMP.tl.4,VAV.fnd.4
CMP.ct.15	Platform standards (Posix, for example)		D	
CMP.ct.16	Test-first programming		D	VAV.tst.1
CMP.tl	*Construction tools*			4	DES.ste.1
CMP.tl.1	Development environments	a	E	
CMP.tl.2	GUI builders	c	E	DES.hci
CMP.tl.3	Unit testing tools	c	E	VAV.tst.1
CMP.tl.4	Application oriented languages (for example, scripting, visual, domain-specific, markup, and macros)	c	E	
CMP.tl.5	Profiling, performance analysis, and slicing tools		D	CMP.ct.14
CMP.fm	*Formal construction methods*			8	DES.dd.9,MAA.af.6,EVO.ac.7
CMP.fm.1	Application of abstract machines (such as SDL and Paisley)	k	E	
CMP.fm.2	Application of specification languages and methods (for example, ASM, B, CSP, VDM, and Z)	a	E	MAA.md.3,MAA.rsd.3
CMP.fm.3	Automatic generation of code from a specification	k	E	
CMP.fm.4	Program derivation	c	E	
CMP.fm.5	Analysis of candidate implementations	c	E	MAA.cf.2
CMP.fm.6	Mapping of a specification to different implementations	k	E	

Reference		k,c,a	E,D,O	Hours	Related Topics
CMP.fm.7	Refinement	c	E		
CMP.fm.8	Proofs of correctness		D		FND.mf.3

4.9 Mathematical and engineering fundamentals

Description

The mathematical and engineering fundamentals of software engineering provide theoretical and scientific underpinnings for constructing software products with desired attributes. These fundamentals support precise descriptions of software engineering products. They provide the mathematical foundations for modeling and facilitating reasoning about these products and their interrelations, and form the basis for a predictable design process. A central theme is engineering design: an iterative decision-making process in which computing, mathematics, and engineering sciences are applied to deploy available resources efficiently to meet a stated objective.

Units and topics

Reference		k,c,a	E,D,O	Hours	Related Topics
FND	**Mathematical and Engineering Fundamentals**			89	
FND.mf	*Mathematical foundations**			56	
FND.mf.1	Functions, relations, and sets (CCCS DS1)	a	E		
FND.mf.2	Basic logic (propositional and predicate) (CCCS DS2)	a	E		MAA.md.2,3
FND.mf.3	Proof techniques (direct, contradiction, inductive) (CCCS DS3)	a	E		CMP.fm.8
FND.mf.4	Basic counting (CCCS DS4)	a	E		
FND.mf.5	Graphs and trees (CCCS DS5)	a	E		CMP.cf.2
FND.mf.6	Discrete probability (CCCS DS6)	a	E		FND.ef.2
FND.mf.7	Finite state machines, regular expressions	c	E		CMP.ct.7,MAA.tm.2
FND.mf.8	Grammars	c	E		CMP.ct.9
FND.mf.9	Numerical precision, accuracy, and errors	c	E		
FND.mf.10	Number theory		D		
FND.mf.11	Algebraic structures		O		
FND.ef	*Engineering foundations for software*			23	
FND.ef.1	Empirical methods and experimental techniques (such as computer-related measuring techniques for CPU and memory usage)	c	E		VAV.fnd.4,VAV.hct.6
FND.ef.2	Statistical analysis (including simple hypothesis testing, estimating, regression, and correlation)	a	E		FND.mf.6
FND.ef.3	Measurement and metrics	k	E		PRO.con.5,PRO.imp.4
FND.ef.4	Systems development (security, safety, performance, effects of scaling, feature interaction, and so on)	k	E		MAA.af.4,DES.con.6,VAV.fnd.4,VAV.tst.9
FND.ef.5	Engineering design (problem formulation, alternative solutions, feasibility, and so on)	c	E		FND.ec.3,MAA.af.1
FND.ef.6	Theory of measurement (for example, criteria for valid measurement)	c	E		
FND.ef.7	Engineering science for other engineering disciplines (strength of materials, digital system principles, logic design, fundamentals of thermodynamics, and so on)		O		
FND.ec	*Engineering economics for software*			10	PRF.pr.6
FND.ec.1	Value considerations throughout the software life cycle	k	E		

Reference		k,c,a	E,D,O		Related Topics
FND.ec.2	Generating system objectives (for example, participatory design, stakeholder win-win, quality function deployment, and prototyping)	c	E		PRF.psy.4,MAA.er.2
FND.ec.3	Evaluating cost-effective solutions (such as benefits realization, tradeoff analysis, cost analysis, and return on investment)	c	E		DES.con.7,MAA.af.4,MGT.pp.4
FND.ec.4	Realizing system value (for example, prioritization, risk resolution, and controlling costs)	k	E		MAA.af.4,MGT.pp.6

* Topics 1-6 correspond to computer science curriculum guidelines for discrete structures 1-6.

4.10 Professional practice

Description

Professional practice is concerned with the knowledge, skills, and attitudes that software engineers must possess to practice software engineering in a professional, responsible, and ethical manner. The study of professional practices includes the areas of technical communication, group dynamics and psychology, and social and professional responsibilities.

Units and topics

Reference		k,c,a	E,D,O	Hours	Related Topics
PRF	**Professional Practice**			35	
PRF.psy	*Group dynamics / psychology*			5	
PRF.psy.1	Dynamics of working in teams/groups	a	E		
PRF.psy.2	Individual cognition (limits, for example)	k	E		DES.hci.10
PRF.psy.3	Cognitive problem complexity	k	E		MAA.rfd.8
PRF.psy.4	Interacting with stakeholders	c	E		FND.ec.2
PRF.psy.5	Dealing with uncertainty and ambiguity	k	E		
PRF.psy.6	Dealing with multicultural environments	k	E		
PRF.com	*Communications skills (specific to SE)*			10	
PRF.com.1	Reading, understanding, and summarizing reading (such as source code and documentation)	a	E		MAA.rsd.1
PRF.com.2	Writing (assignments, reports, evaluations, justifications, and so on)	a	E		
PRF.com.3	Team and group communication (both oral and written, e-mail, and so on)	a	E		MGT.per
PRF.com.4	Presentation skills	a	E		
PRF.pr	*Professionalism*			20	
PRF.pr.1	Accreditation, certification, and licensing	k	E		
PRF.pr.2	Codes of ethics and professional conduct	c	E		
PRF.pr.3	Social, legal, historical, and professional issues and concerns	c	E		
PRF.pr.4	The nature and role of professional societies	k	E		
PRF.pr.5	The nature and role of software engineering standards	k	E		MAA.rsd.1,CMP.ct.14,PRO.imp.3,7,QUA.std
PRF.pr.6	The economic impact of software	c	E		FND.ec
PRF.pr.7	Employment contracts	k	E		

4.11 Software modeling and analysis

Description

Modeling and analysis can be considered core concepts in any engineering discipline because they are essential to documenting and evaluating design decisions and alternatives. Modeling and analysis is first applied to the analysis, specification, and validation of requirements. Requirements represent the real-world needs of users, customers, and other stakeholders affected by the system. The construction of requirements includes an analysis of the desired system's feasibility, elicitation and analysis of stakeholders' needs, the creation of a precise description of what the system should and should not do, along with any constraints on its operation and implementation, and the stakeholders' validation of this description or specification.

Units and Topics

Reference		k,c,a	E,D,O	Hours	Related Topics
MAA	Software Modeling and Analysis			53	
MAA.md	Modeling foundations			19	PRO.con.3,QUA.pro.1,QUA.pda.3
MAA.md.1	Modeling principles (for example, decomposition, abstraction, generalization, projection/views, explicitness, and use of formal approaches)	a	E		CMP.cf.4
MAA.md.2	Pre and post conditions, invariants	c	E		CMP.ct.5
MAA.md.3	Introduction to mathematical models and specification languages (Z and VDM, for example)	c	E		MAA.rsd.3,CMP.fm.2
MAA.md.4	Properties of modeling languages	k	E		
MAA.md.5	Syntax versus semantics (understanding model representations)	c	E		CMP.cf.9
MAA.md.6	Explicitness (make no assumptions or state all assumptions)	k	E		
MAA.tm	Types of models			12	MAA.md
MAA.tm.1	Information modeling (entity-relationship modeling, class diagrams, and so on)	a	E		MAA.rsd.3,DES.dd.5
MAA.tm.2	Behavioral modeling (structured analysis, state diagrams, use-case analysis, interaction diagrams, failure modes and effects analysis, fault tree analysis, and so on)	a	E		FND.mf.7,MAA.er.2,MAA.rsd.3,DES.dd.5
MAA.tm.3	Structure modeling (for example, architectural)	c	E		MAA.rfd.7
MAA.tm.4	Domain modeling (for example, domain engineering approaches)	k	E		
MAA.tm.5	Functional modeling (such as component diagrams)	c	E		
MAA.tm.6	Enterprise modeling (for example, business processes, organizations, and goals)		D		
MAA.tm.7	Modeling embedded systems (for example, real-time schedulability analysis, external interface analysis)		D		
MAA.tm.8	Requirements interaction analysis (for example, feature interaction, house of quality, and viewpoint analysis)		D		
MAA.tm.9	Analysis patterns (for example problem frames and specification re-use)		D		
MAA.af	Analysis fundamentals			6	
MAA.af.1	Analyzing well-formedness (such as completeness, consistency, and robustness)	a	E		
MAA.af.2	Analyzing correctness (such as static analysis, simulation, and model checking)	a	E		
MAA.af.3	Analyzing quality (nonfunctional) requirements (such as safety, security, usability, performance, and root cause analysis)	a	E		FND.ef.4,QUA.pda,DES.con.6,VAV.fnd.4,VAV.tst.9,V

					AV.hct,EVO.ac.4
MAA.af.4	Prioritization, tradeoff analysis, risk analysis, and impact analysis	c	E		FND.ec.3,4,QUA.pda.4
MAA.af.5	Traceability	c	E		DES.ar.4,EVO.pro.2
MAA.af.6	Formal analysis	k	E		CMP.fm
MAA.rfd	*Requirements fundamentals*		.	3	
MAA.rfd.1	Definition of requirements (product, project, constraints, system boundary, external, internal, and so on)	c	E		
MAA.rfd.2	Requirements process	c	E		PRO.con.3
MAA.rfd.3	Layers/levels of requirements (needs, goals, user requirements, system requirements, software requirements, and so on)	c	E		MAA.rsd
MAA.rfd.4	Requirements characteristics (testable, nonambiguous, consistent, correct, traceable, priority, and so on)	c	E		MAA.af.5
MAA.rfd.5	Managing changing requirements	c	E		MGT.ctl.1
MAA.rfd.6	Requirements management (consistency management, release planning, reuse, and so on)	k	E		CMP.ct.3
MAA.rfd.7	Interaction between requirements and architecture	k	E		MAA.tm.3,DES.ar.4,EVO.pro.2
MAA.rfd.8	Relationship of requirements to systems engineering, human-centered design, and so on		D		CMP.cf.6
MAA.rfd.9	Wicked problems (ill-structured problems and problems with many solutions, for example)		D		PRF.psy.3
MAA.rfd.10	COTS as a constraint		D		
MAA.er	*Eliciting requirements*			4	
MAA.er.1	Elicitation sources (stakeholders, domain experts, operational and organization environments, and so on)	c	E		PRF.psy.4
MAA.er.2	Elicitation techniques (interviews, questionnaires/surveys, prototypes, use cases, observation, participatory techniques, and so on)	c	E		FND.ec.2,MAA.er.1, PRF.psy.5
MAA.er.3	Advanced techniques (for example, ethnographic and knowledge elicitation)		O		
MAA.rsd	*Requirements specification and documentation*			6	
MAA.rsd.1	Requirements documentation basics (such as types, audience, structure, quality, attributes, and standards)	k	E		PRF.pr.5
MAA.rsd.2	Software requirements specification	a	E		
MAA.rsd.3	Specification languages (for example, structured English, UML, formal languages such as Z, VDM, SCR, and RSML)	k	E		MAA.md.3,CMP.fm.2
MAA.rv	*Requirements validation*			3	
MAA.rv.1	Reviews and inspection	a	E		VAV.rev
MAA.rv.2	Prototyping to validate requirements (summative prototyping)	k	E		
MAA.rv.3	Acceptance test design	c	E		VAV.tst.8
MAA.rv.4	Validating product quality attributes	c	E		QUA.cc.5
MAA.rv.5	Formal requirements analysis		D		MAA.af.1

4.12 Software design

Description

Software design is concerned with the issues, techniques, strategies, representations, and patterns used to determine the implementation of a component or a system. The design will conform to functional requirements within the constraints imposed by other requirements, such as resource, performance, reliability, and security. This area also includes specification of internal interfaces among software components, architectural design, data design, user interface design, design tools, and design evaluation.

Units and Topics

Reference		k,c,a	E,D,O	Hours	Related Topics
DES	**Software Design**			45	
DES.con	*Design concepts*			3	
DES.con.1	Definition of design	c	E		
DES.con.2	Fundamental design issues (such as persistent data, storage management, and exceptions)	c	E		CMP.ct.6,VAV.tst.2,CMP.cf.11
DES.con.3	Context of design within multiple software development life cycles	k	E		
DES.con.4	Design principles (information hiding, cohesion, and coupling)	a	E		
DES.con.5	Interactions between design and requirements	c	E		DES.ar.4
DES.con.6	Design for quality attributes (reliability, usability, maintainability, performance, testability, security, fault tolerance, and so on)	k	E		FND.ef.4,MAA.tm.4,DES.ar.2,CMP.ct.14,VAV.fnd.4
DES.con.7	Design trade-offs	k	E		FND.ec.3,DES.ar.2,DES.ev
DES.con.8	Architectural styles, patterns, reuse	c	E		DES.ar,DES.dd.2,CMP.ct.3
DES.str	*Design strategies*			6	
DES.str.1	Function-oriented design	a | c	E		
DES.str.2	Object-oriented design	c | a	E		CMP.cf.9,DES.dd.5,CMP.ct.4
DES.str.3	Data-structure centered design		D		
DES.str.4	Aspect-oriented design		O		
DES.ar	*Architectural design*			9	
DES.ar.1	Architectural styles (pipe-and-filter, layered, transaction-centered, peer-to-peer, publish-subscribe, event-based, client-server, and so on)	a	E		DES.con.8
DES.ar.2	Architectural trade-offs between various attributes	a	E		FND.ec.3
DES.ar.3	Hardware issues in software architecture	k	E		CMP.ct.13
DES.ar.4	Requirements traceability in architecture	k	E		MAA.af.5,DES.con.5,EVO.pro.2
DES.ar.5	Domain-specific architectures and product-lines	k	E		
DES.ar.6	Architectural notations (architectural structure viewpoints and representations, component diagrams, and so on)	c	E		MAA.tm
DES.hci	*Human–computer interface design*			12	CMP.cf.7,VAV.hct,CMP.ct.2
DES.hci.1	General HCI design principles	a	E		
DES.hci.2	Use of modes, navigation	a	E		
DES.hci.3	Coding techniques and visual design (color, icons, fonts, and so	c	E		

Reference		k,c,a	E,D,O	Hours	Related Topics
	on)				
DES.hci.4	Response time and feedback	a	E		
DES.hci.5	Design modalities (menu-driven, forms, question-answering, and so on)	a	E		
DES.hci.6	Localization and internationalization	c	E		CMP.ct.8
DES.hci.7	Human–computer interface design methods	c	E		
DES.hci.8	Multimedia (for example, I/O techniques, voice, natural language, Web page, and sound)		D		
DES.hci.9	Metaphors and conceptual models		D		
DES.hci.10	Psychology of HCI		D		PRF.psy.2
DES.dd	*Detailed design*			12	
DES.dd.1	One selected design method (such as SSA/SD, JSD, and OOD)	a	E		
DES.dd.2	Design patterns	a	E		DES.con.8
DES.dd.3	Component design	a	E		CMP.ct.11
DES.dd.4	Component and system interface design	a	E		CMP.ct.2
DES.dd.5	Design notations (class and object diagrams, UML, state diagrams, and so on)	c	E		MAA.tm
DES.ste	*Design support tools and evaluation*			3	
DES.ste.1	Design support tools (such as architectural, static analysis, and dynamic evaluation)	a	E		CMP.ct
DES.ste.2	Measures of design attributes (such as coupling, cohesion, information-hiding, and separation of concerns)	k	E		
DES.ste.3	Design metrics (such as architectural factors, interpretation, and metric sets in common use)	a	E		
DES.ste.4	Formal design analysis		O		MAA.af.2

4.13 Software verification and validation

Description

Software verification and validation uses both static and dynamic system-checking techniques to ensure that the resulting program satisfies its specification and that the program as implemented meets the expectations of the stakeholders. Static techniques are concerned with the analysis and checking of system representations throughout all stages of the software life cycle, whereas dynamic techniques involve only the implemented system.

Units and Topics

Reference		k,c,a	E,D,O	Hours	Related Topics
VAV	**Software Verification and Validation**			42	
VAV.fnd	*V&V terminology and foundations*			5	
VAV.fnd.1	Objectives and constraints of V&V	k	E		
VAV.fnd.2	Planning the V&V effort	k	E		
VAV.fnd.3	Documenting V&V strategy, including tests and other artifacts	a	E		
VAV.fnd.4	Metrics and measurement (reliability, usability, performance, and so on)	k	E		FND.ef.4,MAA.af.2,DES.con.6,CMP.ct.14,PRO.con.4
VAV.fnd.5	V&V involvement at different points in the life cycle	k	E		
VAV.rev	*Reviews*			6	MAA.rv.1
VAV.rev.1	Desk checking	a	E		

VAV.rev.2	Walkthroughs	a	E		
VAV.rev.3	Inspections	a	E		VAV.hct.2,3
VAV.tst	*Testing*			21	MAA.rfd.4,DES.con.6,CMP.ct.15
VAV.tst.1	Unit testing	a	E		CMP.ct.15,CMP.ct.3
VAV.tst.2	Exception handling (writing test cases to trigger exception handling, designing good handling)	a	E		DES.con.2,CMP.ct.6
VAV.tst.3	Coverage analysis and structure-based testing (for example, statement, branch, basis path, multicondition, and data flow)	a	E		
VAV.tst.4	Black-box functional testing techniques	a	E		
VAV.tst.5	Integration testing	c	E		
VAV.tst.6	Developing test cases based on use cases and/or customer stories	a	E		MAA.tm.2
VAV.tst.7	Operational profile-based testing	k	E		
VAV.tst.8	System and acceptance testing	a	E		MAA.rv.4
VAV.tst.9	Testing across quality attributes (for example, usability, security, compatibility, and accessibility)	a	E		MAA.af.3,MAA.rv.6,VAV.hct,QUA.cc.5
VAV.tst.10	Regression testing	c	E		
VAV.tst.11	Testing tools	a	E		CMP.ct.3
VAV.tst.12	Deployment process		D		
VAV.hct	*Human–computer user interface testing and evaluation*			6	DES.hci,VAV.tst.9
VAV.hct.1	The variety of usefulness and usability aspects	k	E		MAA.af.3
VAV.hct.2	Heuristic evaluation	a	E		VAV.rev.3
VAV.hct.3	Cognitive walkthroughs	c	E		VAV.rev.3
VAV.hct.4	User testing approaches (observation sessions and so on)	a	E		
VAV.hct.5	Web usability, testing techniques for Web sites	c	E		
VAV.hct.6	Formal experiments to test hypotheses about specific HCI controls		D		FND.ef.1
VAV.par	*Problem analysis and reporting*			4	
VAV.par.1	Analyzing failure reports	c	E		
VAV.par.2	Debugging/fault isolation techniques	a	E		
VAV.par.3	Defect analysis	k	E		
VAV.par.4	Problem tracking	c	E		

4.14 Software evolution

Description

Software evolution is the result of the ongoing need to support the stakeholders' mission in the face of changing assumptions, problems, requirements, architectures, and technologies. Evolution is intrinsic to all real-world software systems. Support for evolution requires numerous activities both before and after each version or upgrade (release) that constitutes the evolving system. Evolution is a broad concept that expands upon the traditional notion of software maintenance.

Units and Topics

Reference		k,c,a	E,D,O	Hours	Related Topics
EVO	**Software Evolution**			10	
EVO.pro	*Evolution processes*			6	
EVO.pro.1	Basic concepts of evolution and maintenance	k	E		
EVO.pro.2	Relationship between evolving entities (assumptions, requirements, architecture, design, code, and so on)	k	E		MAA.af.4,DES.ar.4
EVO.pro.3	Models of software evolution (theories, laws, and so on)	k	E		
EVO.pro.4	Cost models of evolution		D		FND.ec.3
EVO.pro.5	Planning for evolution (outsourcing, in-house, and so on)		D		MGT.pp
EVO.ac	Evolution activities			4	VAV.par.4,MGT.cm
EVO.ac.1	Working with legacy systems (for example, use of wrappers)	k	E		
EVO.ac.2	Program comprehension and reverse engineering	k	E		
EVO.ac.3	System and process re-engineering (technical and business)	k	E		
EVO.ac.4	Impact analysis	k	E		
EVO.ac.5	Migration (technical and business)	k	E		
EVO.ac.6	Refactoring	k	E		
EVO.ac.7	Program transformation		D		
EVO.ac.8	Data reverse engineering		D		

4.15 Software process

Description

Software process is concerned with knowledge about the description of commonly used software lifecycle process models and the contents of institutional process standards; definition, implementation, measurement, management, change, and improvement of software processes; and use of a defined process to perform the technical and managerial activities needed for software development and maintenance.

Units and Topics

Reference		k,c,a	E,D,O	Hours	Related Topics
PRO	**Software Process**			13	
PRO.con	*Process concepts*			3	
PRO.con.1	Themes and terminology	k	E		
PRO.con.2	Software engineering process infrastructure (for example, personnel, tools, and training)	k	E		
PRO.con.3	Modeling and specification of software processes	c	E		MAA.rfd.2
PRO.con.4	Measurement and analysis of software processes	c	E		MGT.ctl.3
PRO.con.5	Software engineering process improvement (individual, team)	c	E		FND.ef.3,PRO.imp.4,5
PRO.con.6	Quality analysis and control (for example, defect prevention, review processes, quality metrics, and root cause analysis)	c	E		MAA.rv.1,VAV.rev,QUA.pda.4
PRO.con.7	Analysis and modeling of software process models		D		
PRO.imp	*Process implementation*			10	
PRO.imp.1	Levels of process definition (for example, organization, project, team, and individual)	k	E		
PRO.imp.2	Lifecycle models (agile, heavyweight, waterfall, spiral, V-Model	c	E		DES.con.3,VAV.f

Reference		k,c,a	E,D,O		Related Topics
	etc.)				nd.5
PRO.imp.3	Lifecycle process models and standards (for example, IEEE and ISO)	c	E		PRF.pr.5,QUA.pro.2
PRO.imp.4	Individual software process (model, definition, measurement, analysis, improvement)	c	E		PRO.con.5
PRO.imp.5	Team process (model, definition, organization, measurement, analysis, improvement)	c	E		PRO.con.5
PRO.imp.6	Process tailoring	k	E		
PRO.imp.7	Requirements for software lifecycle process (such as ISO/IEEE Standard 12207)	k	E		PRF.pr.5

4.16 Software quality

Description

Software quality is a pervasive concept that affects, and is affected by, all aspects of software development, support, revision, and maintenance. It encompasses the quality of work products developed and/or modified (both intermediate and deliverable work products) and the quality of the work processes used to develop and/or modify the work products. Quality work product attributes include functionality, usability, reliability, safety, security, maintainability, portability, efficiency, performance, and availability.

Units and Topics

Reference		k,c,a	E,D,O	Hours	Related Topics
QUA	**Software Quality**			16	
QUA.cc	*Software quality concepts and culture*			2	
QUA.cc.1	Definitions of quality	k	E		
QUA.cc.2	Society's concern for quality	k	E		
QUA.cc.3	Costs and impacts of bad quality	k	E		
QUA.cc.4	Cost of quality model	c	E		MGT.pp.4
QUA.cc.5	Software quality attributes (for example, dependability and usability)	k	E		MAA.rva.5,VAV.tst.9,QUA.pda.5
QUA.cc.6	Dimensions of quality engineering	k	E		
QUA.cc.7	Roles of people, processes, methods, tools, and technology	k	E		
QUA.std	*Software quality standards*			2	PRF.pr.5
QUA.std.1	ISO 9000 Quality Management Systems	k	E		
QUA.std.2	ISO/IEEE Standard 12207 Software Lifecycle Processes	k	E		
QUA.std.3	Organizational implementation of standards	k	E		
QUA.std.4	IEEE software quality-related standards		D		
QUA.pro	*Software quality processes*			4	
QUA.pro.1	Software quality models and metrics	c	E		VAV.fnd.4,QUA.pda.5
QUA.pro.2	Quality-related aspects of software process models	k	E		PRO.imp.3
QUA.pro.3	Introduction/overview of ISO 15504 and the SEI CMMs	k	E		PRF.pr.5
QUA.pro.4	Quality-related process areas of ISO 15504	k	E		PRF.pr.5
QUA.pro.5	Quality-related process areas of the SW-CMM and the CMMIs	k	E		
QUA.pro.6	Baldrige Award criteria as applied to software engineering		O		
QUA.pro.7	Quality aspects of other process models		O		
QUA.pca	*Process assurance*			4	

Reference		k,c,a	E,D,O	Hours	Related Topics
QUA.pca.1	The nature of process assurance	k	E		
QUA.pca.2	Quality planning	a	E		MGT.pp
QUA.pca.3	Organizing and reporting for process assurance	a	E		
QUA.pca.4	Techniques of process assurance	c	E		
QUA.pda	*Product assurance*			4	
QUA.pda.1	The nature of product assurance	k	E		
QUA.pda.2	Distinctions between assurance and V&V	k	E		VAV
QUA.pda.3	Quality product models	k	E		
QUA.pda.4	Root cause analysis and defect prevention	c	E		PRO.con.6
QUA.pda.5	Quality product metrics and measurement	c	E		VAV.fnd.4,QUA.cc.5,QUA.pro.1
QUA.pda.6	Assessment of product quality attributes (usability, reliability, availability, and so on)	c	E		

4.17 Software management

Description

Software management is concerned with knowledge about the planning, organization, and monitoring of all software lifecycle phases. Management is critical to ensuring that software development projects are appropriate to an organization, work in different organizational units is coordinated, software versions and configurations are maintained, resources are available when necessary, project work is divided appropriately, communication is facilitated, and progress is accurately charted.

Units and Topics

Reference		k,c,a	E,D,O	Hours	Related Topics
MGT	**Software Management**			19	
MGT.con	*Management concepts*			2	
MGT.con.1	General project management	k	E		
MGT.con.2	Classic management models	k	E		
MGT.con.3	Project management roles	k	E		
MGT.con.4	Enterprise/organizational management structure	k	E		
MGT.con.5	Software management types (acquisition, project, development, maintenance, risk, and so on)	k	E		FND.ec.4,MGT.pp.6,EVO
MGT.pp	*Project planning*			6	VAV.fnd.2,QUA.pca.2
MGT.pp.1	Evaluation and planning	c	E		
MGT.pp.2	Work breakdown structure	a	E		
MGT.pp.3	Task scheduling	a	E		
MGT.pp.4	Effort estimation	a	E		FND.ec.3,QUA.cc.4
MGT.pp.5	Resource allocation	c	E		
MGT.pp.6	Risk management	a	E		FND.ec.4
MGT.per	*Project personnel and organization*			2	PRF.com.3
MGT.per.1	Organizational structures, positions, responsibilities, and authority	k	E		PRF.psy.1
MGT.per.2	Formal/informal communication	k	E		PRF.com.1, PRF.com.2, PRF.com.3

MGT.per.3	Project staffing	k	E		
MGT.per.4	Personnel training, career development, and evaluation	k	E		
MGT.per.5	Meeting management	a	E		
MGT.per.6	Building and motivating teams	a	E		
MGT.per.7	Conflict resolution	a	E		
MGT.ctl	*Project control*			4	
MGT.ctl.1	Change control	k	E		MAA.rfd.5,MGT.cm.1,2
MGT.ctl.2	Monitoring and reporting	c	E		
MGT.ctl.3	Measurement and analysis of results	c	E		PRO.con.4
MGT.ctl.4	Correction and recovery	k	E		
MGT.ctl.5	Reward and discipline		O		
MGT.ctl.6	Performance standards		O		
MGT.cm	*Software configuration management*			5	
MGT.cm.1	Revision control	a	E		MGT.ctl.1
MGT.cm.2	Release management	c	E		MGT.ctl.1
MGT.cm.3	Tool support	c	E		
MGT.cm.4	Builds	c	E		
MGT.cm.5	Software configuration management processes	k	E		
MGT.cm.6	Maintenance issues	k	E		EVO.ac
MGT.cm.7	Distribution and backup		D		

4.18 Systems and application specialties

Undergraduate software engineering students should specialize in one or more areas. Within their specialty, students should learn material well beyond the core material specified above. They can specialize in one or more of the 10 knowledge areas listed above, or they can specialize in one or more of the application areas listed below. For each application area, students should obtain breadth of knowledge in the related domain while they obtain depth of knowledge about a particular system's design. Students should also learn the characteristics of typical products in these areas and how these characteristics influence a system's design and construction. Following each application specialty listed below is a set of related topics that are needed to support the application.

This list of application areas is not intended to be exhaustive but is designed to give guidance to those developing specialty curricula.

Specialties and Their Related Topics

Reference	
SAS	**System and Application Specialties**
SAS.net	*Network-centric systems*
SAS.net.1	Knowledge and skills in Web-based technology
SAS.net.2	Depth in networking
SAS.net.3	Depth in security
SAS.inf	*Information systems and data processing*
SAS.inf.1	Depth in databases

SAS.inf.2	Depth in business administration
SAS.inf.3	Data warehousing

SAS.fin	*Financial and e-commerce systems*
SAS.fin.1	Accounting
SAS.fin.2	Finance
SAS.fin.3	Depth in security

SAS.sur	*Fault-tolerant and survivable systems*
SAS.sur.1	Knowledge and skills in heterogeneous, distributed systems
SAS.sur.2	Depth in security
SAS.sur.3	Failure analysis and recovery
SAS.sur.4	Intrusion detection

SAS.sec	*Highly secure systems*
SAS.sec.1	Security-related business issues
SAS.sec.2	Security weaknesses and risks
SAS.sec.3	Cryptography, cryptanalysis, steganography, and so on
SAS.sec.4	Depth in networks

SAS.sfy	*Safety-critical systems*
SAS.sfy.1	Depth in formal methods, proofs of correctness, and so on
SAS.sfy.2	Knowledge of control systems
SAS.sfy.3	Depth in failure modes, effects analysis, and fault tree analysis

SAS.emb	*Embedded and real-time systems*
SAS.emb.1	Hardware for embedded systems
SAS.emb.2	Language and tools for development
SAS.emb.3	Depth in timing issues
SAS.emb.3	Hardware verification

SAS.bio	*Biomedical systems*
SAS.bio.1	Biology and related sciences
SAS.bio.2	Related safety-critical systems knowledge

SAS.sci	*Scientific systems*
SAS.sci.1	Depth in related science
SAS.sci.2	Depth in statistics
SAS.sci.3	Visualization and graphics

SAS.tel	*Telecommunications systems*
SAS.tel.1	Depth in signals, information theory, and so on
SAS.tel.2	Telephony and telecommunications protocols

SAS.av	*Avionics and vehicular systems*
SAS.av.1	Mechanical engineering concepts
SAS.av.2	Related safety-critical systems knowledge
SAS.av.3	Related embedded and real-time systems knowledge

SAS.ind	*Industrial process control systems*
SAS.ind.1	Control systems
SAS.ind.2	Industrial engineering and other relevant engineering areas
SAS.ind.3	Related embedded and real-time systems knowledge

SAS.mm	*Multimedia, game, and entertainment systems*	
SAS.mm.1	Visualization, haptics, and graphics	
SAS.mm.2	Depth in human–computer interface design	
SAS.mm.3	Depth in networks	

SAS.mob	*Systems for small and mobile platforms*	
SAS.mob.1	Wireless technology	
SAS.mob.2	Depth in human–computer interfaces for small and mobile platforms	
SAS.mob.3	Related embedded and real-time systems knowledge	
SAS.mob.4	Related telecommunications systems knowledge	

SAS.ab	Agent-based systems	
SAS.ab.1	Machine learning	
SAS.ab.2	Fuzzy logic	
SAS.ab.3	Knowledge engineering	

Chapter 5:   Guidelines for SE Curriculum Design and Delivery

Chapter 4 of this document presents the SEEK, which includes the knowledge that software engineering graduates need to have. However, *how* the SEEK topics are taught might be as important as *what* is taught. This chapter describes a series of guidelines that should be considered by those developing undergraduate SE curriculums and those teaching individual SE courses.

5.1   Guideline for developing and teaching the curriculum

Curriculum guideline 1: Curriculum designers and instructors must have sufficient relevant knowledge and experience and understand the character of software engineering.

Curriculum designers and instructors should have engaged in scholarship in the broad area of software engineering. This implies

- having software engineering knowledge in most areas of SEEK;

- obtaining real-world experience in software engineering;

- becoming recognized publicly as knowledgeable in software engineering either by having a track record of publication or being active in an appropriate professional society;

- increasing their exposure to the continually expanding variety of software engineering application domains (such as other branches of engineering or business applications), while not claiming expertise in those domains; and

- possessing the motivation and the wherewithal to keep up-to-date with developments in the discipline.

Failure to adhere to this principle will open a program or course to certain risks:

- A program or course might be biased excessively to one kind of software or class of methods, thus not giving students a broad enough exposure to the field, or giving them an inaccurate perception of the field. For example, instructors who have experienced only real-time or only data-processing systems risk flavoring their programs excessively toward these systems. Although it is not bad to have programs that are specialized toward specific types of software engineering, these specializations should be explicitly acknowledged in course titles. Also, in a program as a whole, students should be exposed to a comprehensive selection of systems and approaches.

- Faculty who have a primarily theoretical computer science background might not adequately convey to students the engineering-oriented aspects of software engineering.

- Faculty from related branches of engineering might deliver a software engineering program or course without a full appreciation of the computer science fundamentals that underlie so much of what software engineers do. In addition, they might not cover software for the wide range of domains beyond engineering to which software engineering can be applied.

- Faculty who have not been involved in the development of large systems might not appreciate the importance of process, quality, evolution, and management (which are SEEK knowledge areas).

- Faculty who have made a research career out of pushing the frontiers of software development might not appreciate the fact that students first need to be taught what they can use in practice and need to understand both practical and theoretical motivations behind what they are taught.

5.2   Guidelines for constructing the curriculum

Curriculum guideline 2: Curriculum designers and instructors must think in terms of outcomes.

Both entire programs and individual courses should include attention to outcomes or learning objectives. These outcomes should also be kept in mind as courses are taught. Thinking in terms of outcomes helps ensure that the material included in the curriculum is relevant and is taught in an appropriate manner and at an appropriate depth.

The SE2004 graduate outcomes (see chapter 2) should be used as a basis for designing and assessing software engineering curricula in general. These can be further specialized for the design of individual courses.

In addition, particular institutions might develop more specialized outcomes (for example, particular abilities in specialized applications areas or deeper abilities in certain SEEK knowledge areas).

Curriculum guideline 3: Curriculum designers must strike an appropriate balance between coverage of material and flexibility to allow for innovation.

There is a tendency among those involved in curriculum design to fill a program or course with extensive lists of things that "absolutely must" be covered, leaving relatively little time for flexibility or deeper (but less broad) coverage.

However, there is also a strong body of opinion that students who are given a foundation in the basics and an awareness of advanced material should be able to fill in many gaps in their education later, perhaps in the workforce, and perhaps on an as-needed basis. This suggests that certain kinds of advanced process-oriented SEEK material, although marked at an "a" (application) level of coverage, could be covered at a "k" level if absolutely necessary to allow for various sorts of curriculum innovation. However, material with deeper technical or mathematical content marked "a" should not be reduced to "k" coverage, because it tends to be much harder to learn on the job.

Curriculum guideline 4: Many SE concepts, principles, and issues should be taught as recurring themes throughout the curriculum to help students develop a software engineering mindset.

Material defined in many SEEK units should be distributed throughout many courses in the curriculum. Generally, early courses should introduce the material, with subsequent courses reinforcing and expanding on the material. In most cases, there should also be courses, or parts of courses, that treat the material in depth.

In addition to ethics and tool use, which other guidelines highlight specifically, the following types of material should be presented, at least in part, as recurring themes:

- Measurement, quantification, and formal or mathematical approaches.

- Modeling, representation, and abstraction.

- Human factors and usability. Students need to repeatedly see that software engineering is not just about technology.

- The fact that many software engineering principles are in fact core engineering principles. Students might learn SE principles better if they witness the same principle in action elsewhere. For example, all engineers use models, measure, solve problems, and use "black boxes."

- The importance of scale. Students can practice only on relatively small problems, yet they need to appreciate that the power of many techniques is most obvious in large systems. They need to be able to practice tasks as if they were working on very large systems, and to practice reading and understanding large systems.

- The importance of reuse

- Much of the material in the Process, Quality, Evolution, and Management knowledge areas.

Curriculum guideline 5: Learning certain software engineering topics requires maturity, so these topics should be taught toward the end of the curriculum, whereas other material should be taught earlier to help students gain that maturity.

It is important to structure the material that has to be taught so students fully appreciate the underlying principles and motivation. If taught too early in the curriculum, many topics from SEEK's Process, Quality, Evolution, and Management knowledge areas are likely to be poorly understood and appreciated by students. This should be taken into account when designing the sequence in which material is to be taught and the process for introducing real-world experiences to the students. It is suggested that introductory material on these topics be taught in early years, with the bulk of the material left to the latter part of the curriculum.

On the other hand, students also need to be taught very practical material early so they can begin to gain maturity by participating in real-world development experiences (in the work force or in student projects). Topics that should be taught beginning early in the curriculum include programming, human factors, aspects of requirements and design, as well as verification and validation. This does not mean to imply that programming must be taught first, as in a traditional CS1 course, but that at least a reasonable amount should be taught in a student's first year.

Students should also be exposed to "difficult" software engineering situations relatively early in their program. Examples of these might be dealing with rapidly changing requirements, having to understand and change a large existing system, having to work in a large team, etc. The concept behind such experiences is to raise awareness in students that process, quality, evolution and management are important things to study, *before* they start studying them.

Curriculum guideline 6: Students must learn some application domain (or domains) outside of software engineering.

Almost all software engineering activity involves solving problems for customers in domains outside software engineering. Therefore, somewhere in their curriculum, students should be able to study one or more outside domains in reasonable depth.

Studying such material will not only give the student direct domain knowledge they can apply to software engineering problems, but will also teach them the domain's language and thought processes, enabling more in-depth study later on.

By "in reasonable depth," we mean one or more courses above the introductory level (at least heavy second-year courses and beyond). The choice of domain (or domains) is a local consideration and in many cases can be at least partly left up to the student. Domains can include other branches of engineering or the natural sciences. They can also include social sciences, business, and the humanities. No one domain should be considered more important to software engineering programs than another.

The study of certain domains might necessitate additional supporting courses, such as particular areas of mathematics and computer science as well as deeper areas of software engineering. The reader should consult the Systems and Application Specialties area at the end of the SEEK (chapter 4) for recommendations for such supporting courses.

This guideline does not preclude the possibility of designing courses or programs that deeply integrate the teaching of domain knowledge with the teaching of software engineering. In fact, such an approach would be innovative and commendable. For example, an institution could have courses called "Telecommunications Software Engineering," "Aerospace Software Engineering," "Information Systems, Software Engineering," or "Software Engineering of Sound and Music Systems." However, in such cases great care must be taken to ensure that the depth is not sacrificed in either SE or the domain. The risk is that the instructor, the instructional material, or the presentation might not have adequate depth in one or the other area.

5.3 Attributes and attitudes that should pervade the curriculum and its delivery

Curriculum guideline 7: Software engineering must be taught in ways that recognize it is both a computing and an engineering discipline.

Educators should develop an appreciation of those aspects of software engineering that it shares with both other branches of engineering and other branches of computing, particularly computer science. Chapter 2 presents characteristics of engineering and computing.

- **Engineering**: Engineering has been evolving for millennia, and a great deal of general wisdom has been built up, although some parts of it need to be adapted to the software engineering context. Software engineering students must come to believe that they are real engineers: They must develop a sense of the engineering ethos, and an understanding of the responsibilities of being an engineer. This can be achieved only by appropriate attitudes on the part of all faculty and administrators.

This principle does not require that software engineers endorse all aspects of the engineering profession. There are those, within and outside the profession, who criticize some aspects of the profession, and their views should be respected with an eye to improving the profession. Also, there are some ways that software engineering differs from other types of engineering (it produces a less tangible product, for example, and has roots in different branches of science), and these must be taken into account. This principle also does not require that a particular model of the profession be adopted.

- **Computing**: For software engineers to have the technical competence to develop high-quality software, they must have a solid and deep background in the fundamentals of computer science, as outlined in chapter 4. That knowledge will ensure that they understand the limits of computing, and the technologies available to undertake a software engineering project.

This principle does not require that a software engineer's knowledge of these areas be as deep as a computer scientist's. However, the software engineer needs to have sufficient knowledge and practice to choose among and apply these technologies appropriately. Software engineers must also have sufficient appreciation for the complexity of these technologies to recognize when they are beyond their area of expertise and when they therefore need to consult a specialist (for example, a database analyst).

Curriculum guideline 8: Students should be trained in certain personal skills that transcend the subject matter.

The following skills tend to be required for almost all activities that students will encounter in the workforce. These skills must be acquired primarily through practice.

- **Exercising critical judgment**: Making a judgment among competing solutions is a key part of being an engineer. Curriculum design and delivery should therefore help students build the knowledge, analytical skills, and methods they need to make sound judgments. Of particular importance is a willingness to think critically. Students should also be taught to judge the reliability of various sources of information.

- **Evaluating and challenging received wisdom:** Students should be trained to not immediately accept everything they are taught or read. They should also gain an understanding of the limitations of current SE knowledge, and how SE knowledge seems to be developing.

- **Recognizing their own limitations**: Students should be taught that professionals consult other professionals and that there is great strength in teamwork.

- **Communicating effectively**: Students should learn to communicate well in all contexts—in writing, when giving presentations, when demonstrating (their own or others') software, and in discussions with others. Students should also build listening, cooperation, and negotiation skills.

- **Behaving ethically and professionally.** Students should learn to think about the ethical, privacy, and security implications of their work. See also guideline 15.

There are some SEEK topics relevant to the above that can be taught in lectures, especially aspects of communication ability; however, students will learn these skills most effectively if they are constantly emphasized though group projects, carefully marked written work, and student presentations.

Curriculum guideline 9: Students should be instilled with the ability and eagerness to learn.

Because so much of what is learned will change over a student's professional career, and because only a small fraction of what could be learned will be taught and learned at university, it is of paramount importance that students develop the habit of continually expanding their knowledge.

Curriculum guideline 10: Software engineering must be taught as a problem-solving discipline.

An important goal of most software projects is solving customers' problems, both explicit and implicit. It is important to recognize this when designing programs and courses: Such recognition focuses the learner on the rationale for what he or she is learning, deepens the understanding of the knowledge learned, and helps ensure that the material taught is relevant. Unfortunately, a common mistake is to focus on purely technical problems, thus leading to systems that are not useful.

There are a variety of classes of problems, all of which are important. Some, such as analysis, design, and testing problems, are product-oriented and are aimed directly at solving the customers' problem. Others, such as process improvement, are metaproblems whose solution will facilitate the product-oriented, problem-solving process. Still others, such as ethical problems, transcend the above two categories.

Problem solving is best learned through practice and taught through example. Having a teacher show a solution on the screen can go part of the way but is never sufficient. Students therefore must be given a significant number of assignments.

Curriculum guideline 11: The underlying and enduring *principles* of software engineering should be emphasized, rather than *details* of the latest or specific tools.

The SEEK lists many topics that can be taught using a variety of computer hardware, software applications, technologies, and processes (which we refer to collectively as tools). In a good curriculum, the enduring knowledge in the SEEK topics are emphasized, not the details of the tools. The topics are supposed to remain valid for many years; as much as possible, the knowledge and experience derived from their learning should still be applicable 10 or 20 years later. Particular tools, on the other hand, will rapidly change. It is a mistake, for example, to focus excessively on how to use a particular vendor's piece of software, on the detailed steps of a methodology, or on a programming language's syntax.

Applying this guideline to languages requires understanding that the line between what is enduring and what is temporary can be somewhat hard to pinpoint and can be a moving target. It is clear, for example, that software engineers should definitely learn in detail several programming languages as well as other types of languages (such as specification languages). This guideline should be interpreted to mean that when learning such languages, students must learn much more than just surface syntax, and, having learned the languages, should be able to learn whatever new languages appear with little difficulty.

Applying this guideline to processes (also known as methods or methodologies') is similar to applying it to languages. Students ought not to have to memorize long lists of steps, but should instead learn the underlying wisdom behind the steps such that they can choose whatever methodologies appear in the future, and can creatively adapt and mix processes.

Applying this guideline to technologies (both hardware and software) means not having to memorize in detail an API, user interface, or instruction set just for the sake of it. Instead, students should develop the skill of looking up details in a reference manual whenever needed, so that they can concentrate on more important matters.

Curriculum guideline 12: The curriculum must be taught so that students gain experience using appropriate and up-to-date tools, even though tool details are not the focus of the learning.

Performing software engineering efficiently and effectively requires choosing and using the most appropriate computer hardware, software tools, technologies, and processes (again, collectively referred to as tools). Students must therefore be habituated to choosing and using tools so that they go into the workforce with this habit—a habit that is often hard to pick up in the workforce, where the pressure to deliver results can often cause people to hesitate to learn new tools.

Appropriateness of tools must be carefully considered. A tool that is too complex, too unreliable, too expensive, too hard to learn given the available time and resources, or provides too little benefit is inappropriate, whether in the educational context or in the work context. Many software engineering tools have failed because they have not met this criterion.

Tools should be selected that support the process of learning principles.

Tools used in curricula must be reasonably up-to-date for several reasons:

- so students can take the tools into the workplace as "ambassadors," performing a form of technology transfer,

- so students can take advantage of the tool skills they have learned,

- so students and employers will not feel that the education is out of-date, even if up-to-date principles are being taught.

Having said that, older tools can sometimes be simpler, and therefore more appropriate for certain needs.

This guideline might seem in conflict with curriculum guideline 11, but that conflict is illusory. The key to avoiding the conflict is recognizing that teaching the use of tools does not mean that the object of the teaching is the tools themselves. Learning to use tools should be a secondary activity performed in laboratory or tutorial sessions, or by the student on his or her own. Students should realize that the tools are only aids, and they should learn not to fear learning new tools.

Curriculum guideline 13: Material taught in a software engineering program should, where possible, be grounded in sound research and mathematical or scientific theory, or else widely accepted good practice.

There must be evidence that whatever is taught is indeed true and useful. This evidence can take the form of validated scientific or mathematical theory (such as in many areas of computer science), or else widely used and generally accepted best practice.

It is important, however, not to be overly dogmatic about the application of theory: It might not always be appropriate. For example, formalizing a specification or design, so as to be able to apply mathematical approaches, can be inefficient and reduce agility in many situations. In other circumstances, however, it can be essential.

In situations in which material taught is based on generally accepted practice that has not yet been scientifically validated, the fact that the material is still open to question should be made clear.

When teaching "good practices," it is important not to present them in a context-free manner, but with examples of the success of the practices and of failure caused by not following them. The same should be true when presenting knowledge derived from research.

This guideline complements curriculum guideline 11. Whereas curriculum guideline 11 stresses focus on fundamental software engineering principles, curriculum guideline 13 says that what is taught should be well founded.

Curriculum guideline 14: The curriculum should have a significant real-world basis.

Incorporating real-world elements into the curriculum is necessary to enable effective learning of software engineering skills and concepts. A program should be set up to incorporate at least some of the following:

- **Case studies**: Exposure to real systems and project case studies, taught to critique them as well as reuse the best parts of them.

- **Project-based classes**: Some courses should be set up to mimic typical projects in industry. These should include group work, presentations, formal reviews, quality assurance, and so on. It can be beneficial if such a course includes a real-world customer or customers. Group projects can be interdisciplinary. Students should also be able to experience the different roles typical in a software engineering team: project manager, tools engineer, requirements engineer, and so on.

- **Capstone course(s)**: Students need a significant project, preferably spanning their entire last year, in order to practice the knowledge and skills they have learned. Unlike project-based classes, the capstone project is managed by the students and solves a problem of the student's choice. Discussion of a capstone course in the curriculum can be found in section 6.3.2. In some locales, group capstone projects are the norm, whereas in others individual capstone projects are required.

- **Practical exercises:** Students should be given practical exercises so they can develop skills in current practices and processes.

- **Student work experience**: Where possible, students should have some form of industrial work experience as a part of their program. This could take the form of one or more internships, co-op work terms, or sandwich work terms (the terminology used here is clearly country-dependent). It is desirable, although not always possible, to make work experience compulsory. If opportunities for work experience are difficult to provide, then simulation of work experience must be achieved in courses.

Even if they incorporate all of these elements, instructors should keep in mind that the level of real-world exposure their students can achieve as an undergraduate will be limited: students will generally come to appreciate the extreme complexity and the true consequences of poor work only by bitter experience as they work on various projects in their careers. Educators can only start the process of helping students develop a mature understanding of the real world, and they must realize that it will be a difficult challenge to enable students to appreciate everything they are taught.

Curriculum guideline 15: Ethical, legal, and economic concerns, and the notion of what it means to be a professional, should be raised frequently.

One of the key reasons for the existence of a defined profession is to ensure that its members follow ethical and professional principles. By taking opportunities to discuss these issues throughout the curriculum, instructors will ensure that they become deeply entrenched. One aspect of this is exposing students to standards and guidelines. See section 2.4 for further discussion of professionalism.

5.4   General strategies for software engineering pedagogy

Curriculum guideline 16: To ensure that students embrace certain important ideas, educators must motivate students by using interesting, concrete, and convincing examples.

It may be only through bitter experience that software engineers learn certain concepts and techniques considered central to the discipline. In some cases, the educational community has not appreciated the value of such concepts and has therefore not taught them. In other cases, educators have encountered skepticism on the part of students.

In these cases, educators must put considerable attention into motivating students to accept the ideas through interesting, concrete, and revealing examples. The examples should be of sufficient size and complexity to demonstrate that using the material being taught has obvious benefits, and that failure to use the material would lead to undesirable consequences.

The following are examples of areas where motivation is particularly needed:

- Mathematical foundations: Logic and discrete mathematics should be taught in the context of its *application* to software engineering or computer science problems. If derivations and proofs are to be presented, they should preferably be taught after the importance of the result is described. Statistics and empirical methods should likewise be taught in an applied, rather than abstract, manner.

- Process and quality: Students must be made aware of the consequences of poor processes and bad quality. They must also be exposed to good processes and quality, so that they can experience for themselves the effect of improvements, feel pride in their work, and learn to appreciate good work.

- Human factors and usability: Students often will not appreciate the need for attention to these areas unless they actually experience usability difficulties, or watch users having difficulty using software.

Curriculum guideline 17: Software engineering education in the 21st century needs to move beyond the lecture format: It is therefore important to encourage consideration of a variety of teaching and learning approaches.

The most common approach to teaching software engineering material is through lectures, supplemented by laboratory sessions, tutorials, and so on. However, alternative approaches can help students learn more effectively. Some approaches that might be considered to supplement or even largely replace the lecture format in certain cases include

- Problem-based learning: This has been found to be particularly useful in other professional disciplines, and is now used to teach engineering in some institutions. See curriculum guideline 10 for a discussion of the problem-solving nature of the discipline.

- Just-in-time learning: Teaching fundamental material immediately before teaching the application of that material. For example, teaching aspects of mathematics the day before applying them in a software engineering context. There is evidence that this helps students retain the fundamental material, although it can be difficult to accomplish because faculty must coordinate across courses.

- Learning by failure: Students are given a task they will have difficulty with. They are then taught methods that would enable them to do the task more easily in the future.

- Self-study materials that students work through on their own schedule, including online and computer-based learning.

Curriculum guideline 18: Important efficiencies and synergies can be achieved by designing curricula so that several types of knowledge are learned at the same time.

Many people browsing through the SEEK have commented that there is a very large amount of material to be taught, or contrarily, that many topics are assigned a rather small number of hours. However, if careful attention is paid to the curriculum, many topics can be taught concurrently. In fact, two topics listed as requiring x and y hours respectively can be taught together in less than $x + y$ hours.

The following are some of the many situations in which such synergistic teaching and learning can be applied:

- Modeling, languages, and notations: Considerable depth in languages such as UML can be achieved by merely using the notation when teaching other concepts. The same applies to formal methods and programming. Clearly, some time will need to be set aside to teach the basics of a language or modeling technique per se, but both broad and deep knowledge can be learned as students study a wide range of other topics.

- Process, quality, and management: Students can be instructed to follow certain processes as they are working on exercises or projects whose explicit objective is to learn other concepts.

In these circumstances, it would be desirable for students to have had some introduction to process, so that they know why they are being asked to follow a process. Also, it might be desirable to follow the exercise or project with a discussion of the usefulness of applying the particular process. The depth of learning of the process is likely to be considerable, with relatively little time taken away from the other material being taught.

- Mathematics: Students might deepen and expand their understanding of statistics while analyzing data resulting from studies of reliability or performance. Opportunities to deepen understanding of logic and other branches of discrete mathematics also abound.

- Teaching multiple concepts at the same time in this manner can, in fact, help students appreciate linkages among topics, and can make material more interesting to them. In both cases, this should lead to better retention of material.

Curriculum guideline 19: Courses and curricula must be reviewed and updated regularly.

Software engineering is rapidly evolving; hence, most (if not all) courses or curricula will, over time, become out of date. Institutions and instructors must therefore regularly review their courses and programs and make whatever changes are necessary. This guideline applies to curricula or courses developed by individual institutions and faculty. On the other hand, principles 3 and 4 in section 3.1 require that SE2004 itself acknowledge the rapid evolution of the field and make necessary changes.

5.5   Concluding Comment

The above represents a set of key guidelines that need to underpin the development of a high-quality software engineering program. They are not necessarily the only concerns. For each institution, there are likely to be local and national needs driven by industry, government, and so on. The aspirations of the students themselves must also be considered. Students must see value in the education, and they must see it meeting their needs. Often, this is conditioned by their achievements (for example, what they have been able to build) during their program and by their career aspirations and options. Certainly, they should feel confident about being able to compete within the global workforce.

Any software engineering curriculum or syllabus needs to integrate all of these considerations into a single, coherent program. Ideally, a uniform and consistent ethos should permeate individual classes and the environment in which the program is delivered. A software engineering program should instill in the student a set of expectations and values associated with engineering high-quality software systems.

Chapter 6: Courses and Course Sequences

This chapter presents a set of example curricula that can be used to teach the knowledge described in the SEEK (chapter 4), according to the guidelines described in chapter 5.

This section is organized as follows. In section 6.1, we describe how we have categorized courses and the coding scheme we use. In the subsequent sections, we discuss patterns for introductory courses, intermediate software engineering courses, and other courses, respectively. Details of the courses, including mappings to SEEK, are left to Appendix A.

This document is intended as a resource for institutions that are developing or improving programs in software engineering at the undergraduate level, as well as for accreditation agencies that need sample curricula to help them make decisions about various institutions' programs. The patterns and course descriptions that follow describe reasonable approaches to designing and delivering programs and courses, but are not intended to be prescriptive nor exhaustive. We do suggest, however, that institutions strongly consider using this chapter as a basis for curriculum design, because similarity among institutions will benefit at least three groups: students wishing to transfer, employers wishing to understand what students know, and the creators of educational materials such as textbook authors.

Even if an institution decides to base their curriculum on those presented here, it should still consider its own local needs and adapt the curriculum as needed. Local issues that will vary from institution to institution include the preparation of the entering students, the availability and expertise of faculty at the institution, the overall culture and goals of the institution, and 4) any additional material that the institution wants its students to learn. Developing a comprehensive set of desired student outcomes for a program (see chapter 2) should be the starting point.

Relationship to CCCS

The *CC2001 Computer Science* volume (CCCS) [IEEE 2001b] contains a set of recommendations for undergraduate programs in computer science. Although undergraduate degrees in software engineering differ from degrees in computer science, the two have much in common, particularly at the introductory levels. We refer to descriptions developed in CCCS when appropriate and show how some of them can be adopted directly. This will be important for many institutions that offer both computer science and software engineering degrees.

How this section was developed

To develop these curricula, a subcommittee of volunteers created a first draft. Numerous iterations followed, with changes largely made by steering committee members as a result of input from various workshops. The original committee members started with SEEK, CCCS, and a survey of 32 existing bachelor's degree programs from North America, Europe, and Australia. A key technique in developing curricula was determining which SEEK topics could be covered by reusing CCCS courses. A key subsequent step was working out ways to distribute the remaining SEEK material into cohesive software engineering courses, using the existing programs as a guide. It should be noted that many of the existing bachelor's degree programs do not, in fact, cover SEEK entirely, so the proposals did not originally match any program exactly. Since the first draft of this document, at least one university has implemented many of the courses in the document. Feedback from that exercise was used to refine the courses shown here.

6.1　Course coding scheme

In this document, we used the following coding scheme for courses:

XXnnn

where,

        XX is one of

                CS—for courses taken from CCCS
                SE—for software engineering courses defined in this document
                NT—for nontechnical courses defined in this document
                MA—for a mathematics course defined in this document

      nnn is an identifying number where

- the first digit indicates the earliest year in a four-year period that the course would typically be taken
- the second digit divides the courses into broad subcategories within SE
  0 means the course is broad, covering many areas of SEEK
  1 means the course is heavily weighted in design and computing fundamentals that are the basis for design
  2 means the course is heavily weighted in process-oriented material
- the third digit distinguishes among courses that would otherwise have the same number

Except where specified, all courses are 40-hour standard courses in the North American model. As discussed earlier, this does not mean that there must be 40 hours of lecturing, but that the amount of material covered is equivalent to a traditional course with 40 hours of lectures, plus twice that time for self-study, labs, tutorials, exams, and so on.

The course identifiers use different shading, font, and labels to distinguish between various categories of courses.

The first category of courses would typically be taught early and represents essential introductory material. The next section discusses specific courses and sequences of courses.

> SE + CS introductory courses—first-year start

> Introductory computer science courses from CCCS

> Mathematics fundamentals courses

The second category of courses primarily covers core software engineering material from SEEK. These are discussed in section 6.3.

> Software engineering core courses

> Capstone project course

The next group of courses covers material that is essential in the curriculum but the group is neither introductory nor core software engineering material. Section 6.4 discusses such courses.

Intermediate fundamental computer science courses

Nontechnical (NT) compulsory courses

The following course categories will be elective and optional in at least some institutions, while perhaps required in others. These are also discussed in section 6.4.

Mathematics courses that are not SE core

Technical elective (Tech elect) courses (SE/CS/IT/CE) that are not SE core

Science/engineering courses covering non-SEEK topics

General nontechnical (Gen ed) courses

Unconstrained (--)

The last category is used when course slots are specified, yet no specific course is specified for the slot.

6.2 Introductory sequences covering software engineering, computer science, and mathematics material

There are several approaches to introducing software engineering to students in the first year-and-a-half of a bachelor's degree program. In this section, we briefly describe the sequences and the courses they include. We initially describe sequences that teach introductory computing material, and then we discuss sequences for teaching mathematics. Full details of new courses, including a formal calendar description, prerequisites, learning objectives, teaching modules, mapping to SEEK, and other material, is found in Appendix A. Appendix A also has a mapping to SEEK of courses borrowed from the CCCS volume.

The distinguishing feature of the two main computing sequences is whether students start with courses that immediately introduce software engineering concepts, or whether they instead start with a pure computer science first year and are only introduced to software engineering in a serious way in the second year. There is no clear evidence regarding which of these approaches is best. The CS-first approach is by far the more common, and, for solid pragmatic reasons, seems likely to remain so. However, some suggest the SE-first approach as a way to ensure that students develop a proper sense of what software engineering is all about. Following are some perceived advantages and disadvantages of the two approaches.

Arguments for the SE-first approach:

- Students are taught from the start to think as software engineers, to focus on the problem to be solved, to consider requirements and design before coding, to think about process, to work iteratively, and to adopt other software engineering practices. In other words, they are taught the habit of thinking about everything required to develop a large system, right from the start.

- Students are less likely to develop the habit of thinking primarily in terms of code, or thinking of code as the objective as opposed to a means to an end. Some feel that this mindset is hard to break later, and leads to students being skeptical of many of the tenets of software engineering. A good CS-first approach can still avoid this, but some people feel that an SE-first approach is likely to more readily avoid it.

- Exposure to SE early will make them feel more comfortable with their choice of discipline.

Arguments for a CS-first approach

- Programming is a fundamental skill required by all software engineers; it is also a skill that takes much practice to become good at. The more and earlier students practice programming, the better they are likely to become. Some would disagree with the importance of programming to a software engineer, but the consensus among those developing this document is that it is an essential skill.

- Students who know little about computers or programming might not be able to grasp SE concepts in first year, or would find that those concepts have little meaning for them.

- There are many textbooks for standard first-year CS courses, and few that take a truly SE-first approach. Teaching in an SE-first manner might therefore require instructors to produce much of their own material.

- Because many institutions offer both SE and CS degrees, they will want to share courses to reduce resource requirements.

- There is a shortage of SE faculty in many institutions. The SE faculty who are available are needed to teach the more advanced courses. Diverting them to teach first year can reduce the quality of later SE courses.

- Most employment open to students after their first year will involve programming. Employers will be reluctant to give students responsibility for design or requirements until they have matured further. Thus, development of programming skills should be emphasized in the first year.

There is clearly some wisdom in both approaches, and little convincing evidence that either is as bad or as good as some people might claim. To strike some middle ground, the courses in both sequences indeed have some material from the "other side." The core CCCS first-year courses have a certain amount of SE coverage, and the first-year courses we propose for the SE-first approach also teach the fundamentals of implementation, although not as deeply as the CS courses.

It is intended that by the time students reach the end of either introductory sequence, they will have covered the same topics.

6.2.1 Introductory computing sequence A: Start software engineering in first year

In this sequence, a student's first year involves two courses, SE101 and SE102 (described later), that introduce software engineering in conjunction with some programming and other computer science concepts. These courses differ from traditional introductory computer science courses in two ways:

- Because of the inclusion of a more in-depth introduction to software engineering, less time is spent on developing programming skills.

- The engineering perspective plays a major role in the course.

Thus, the impact of a few extra hours formally devoted to software engineering is multiplied through an emphasis on using a software engineering approach in all programming assignments.

In second year, students take courses CS103 and SE200, which prepare them for the intermediate sequences discussed in section 6.3. CS103 and SE200 combine to finish the development of basic computing knowledge and programming skills in the students in the program. SE200 contains some of the programming-oriented material normally found in introductory computing courses but not included in SE101 and SE102. CS103 and SE200 can be taken concurrently or one before the other. For scheduling purposes, it is often best if they are taken at the same time.

Following are brief descriptions of these courses.

SE101 Introduction to Software Engineering and Computing

A first course in software engineering and computing for the software engineering student who has taken no prior computer science courses at the university level. Introduces fundamental programming concepts as well as basic concepts of software engineering.

SE102 Software Engineering and Computing II

A second course in software engineering, delving deeper into software engineering concepts, while continuing to introduce computer science fundamentals.

SE200 Software Engineering and Computing III

Continues a broad introduction to software engineering and computing concepts.

CS103 Data Structures and Algorithms

Any variant of CS103 from the CCCS can be used (for example, those from the imperative-first or objects-first sequences). Normally, this course has CS102 as a prerequisite; in this sequence, SE102 is the prerequisite. The CCCS volume describes the course as follows:

Builds on the foundation provided by the CS101-102I sequence to introduce the fundamental concepts of data structures and the algorithms that proceed from them. Topics include recursion, the underlying philosophy of object-oriented programming, fundamental data structures (including stacks, queues, linked lists, hash tables, trees, and graphs), the basics of algorithmic analysis, and an introduction to the principles of language translation.

6.2.2 Introductory computing sequence B: Introduction to software engineering in second year

In this sequence, a student starts with one of the initial sequences of computer science courses specified in the CCCS volume for CS degrees. Specialization in software engineering starts in second year with SE201, which can be taken at the same time as the third CS course.

The CCCS volume offers several variants of the CS introductory courses. Any of these can be used, although the imperative-first (subscript I), and objects-first (subscript O) seem the best foundations for software engineering. CS103 was described in the last subsection; the imperative-first versions of the first two CS courses, along with SE201-int are briefly described below and in Appendix A. Note that CS101 and CS102 cover mostly computing fundamentals topics from SEEK, but also cover small amounts of software engineering material from other SEEK knowledge areas. Even with the inclusion of the basics of software engineering, it is not expected that software engineering practices will be strongly emphasized in the programming assignments.

The CCCS volume also allows for a "compressed" introduction to computer science, in which CS101, CS102, and CS103 are taught as a two-course sequence CS111 and CS112. If such courses are used in software engineering degrees, coverage of SEEK will bc insufficient unless students are admitted with some CS background or extra CS coverage is added to other courses.

CS101I Programming Fundamentals

This is a standard introduction to computer science, using an imperative-first approach. The description from the CCCS volume is:

Introduces the fundamental concepts of procedural programming. Topics include data types, control structures, functions, arrays, files, and the mechanics of running, testing, and debugging. The course also offers an introduction to the historical and social context of computing and an overview of computer science as a discipline.

CS102I The Object-Oriented Paradigm

This is the second in a standard sequence of introductory CS courses. The description from the CCCS volume is:

Introduces the concepts of object-oriented programming to students with a background in the procedural paradigm. The course begins with a review of control structures and data types with emphasis on structured data types and array processing. It then moves on to introduce the object-oriented programming paradigm, focusing on the definition and use of classes along with the fundamentals of object-oriented design. Other topics include an overview of programming language principles, simple analysis of algorithms, basic searching and sorting techniques, and an introduction to software engineering issues.

SE201 Introduction to Software Engineering

This is a central course, presenting the basic principles and concepts of software engineering and giving a firm foundation for many other courses described below. It gives broad coverage of the most important terminology and concepts in software engineering. After completing this course, students will be able to do basic modeling and design, particularly using UML. They will also have a basic understanding of requirements, software architecture, and testing.

6.2.3 Introductory mathematics sequences

Discrete mathematics is the mathematics underlying all computing, including software engineering. It has the importance to software engineering that calculus has to other branches of engineering. Statistics and empirical methods also are of key importance to software engineering.

The mathematics fundamentals courses cover SEEK's FND.mf topic and some of FND.ef—that is, discrete mathematics plus probability, statistics, and empirical methods. We have reused CCCS courses CS105 and CS106. Because the CS volume lacks an appropriate course covering certain SEEK material, we have created a new course MA271 to cover statistics and empirical methods.

It is recommended that these courses be taught starting in first year, although that is not strictly necessary. This material is needed for some, but not all, of the intermediate software engineering courses discussed in the next section.

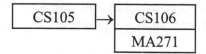

CS105 Discrete Structures I

Standard first course in discrete mathematics. Taught in a way that shows how the material can be applied to software and hardware design. The description from the CS volume is as follows:

Introduces the foundations of discrete mathematics as they apply to computer science, focusing on providing a solid theoretical foundation for further work. Topics include functions, relations, sets, simple proof techniques, Boolean algebra, propositional logic, digital logic, elementary number theory, and the fundamentals of counting.

CS106 Discrete Structures II

Standard second course in discrete mathematics. The description from the CS volume is as follows:

Continues the discussion of discrete mathematics introduced in CS105. Topics in the second course include predicate logic, recurrence relations, graphs, trees, matrices, computational complexity, elementary computability, and discrete probability.

MA271 Statistics and Empirical Methods

Applied probability and statistics in the context of computing. Experiment design and the analysis of results. The course is taught using examples from software engineering and other computing disciplines.

6.3 Core software engineering sequences

In this section, we present two sequences, each containing six intermediate software engineering courses. We also present the capstone course. Full details of the new courses, including a formal calendar description, prerequisites, learning objectives, teaching modules, mapping to SEEK, and other material, can be found in Appendix A.

None of the courses in these sequences are fully specified (that is, none have all of the 40 hours allocated to topics). This allows institutions and instructors to be flexible as they adapt the courses to their needs.

The reasons for having two packages are the following:

- Some institutions may have existing courses that fit one of the packages and that they would like to reuse as much as possible. For example, package I has a requirements course, whereas Package II distributes this material in other courses. Package II, on the other hand, has a pure testing course, whereas Package I instead has a course that covers both testing and quality assurance.

- There may be individual or institutional preferences for organizing material in one way or another. For example, while some like having a formal methods course as a separate entity (Package II), others distinctly do not (Package I).

No matter which package is chosen, coverage of essential SEEK topics at the end will be the same. However, coverage of desirable and optional topics, as well as those topics added by each institution, will differ somewhat.

Both six-course sequences have either SE201-int or SE 200 as prerequisites, and would normally be started in second year. Also, both sequences contain SE212. In both sequences, the courses are labeled (A), (B), …, (F). These letters are used in the course patterns discussed in section 6.5; they indicate the slots into which the courses can be placed.

Indentation from the left margin means that a course should not be taken too early in the curriculum since it requires maturity, but that there is no explicit prerequisite preventing it from being taken early.

6.3.1 Core Software Engineering Package I

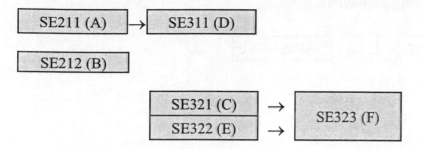

The following are titles and brief summaries of the courses in this package.

SE211 Software Construction

Covers low-level design issues, including formal approaches.

SE212 Software Engineering Approach to Human–Computer Interaction

Covers a wide variety of topics relating to designing and evaluating user interfaces, as well as some of the psychological background needed to understand people. This course is also found in Core Software Engineering Package II.

SE311 Software Design and Architecture

Covers advanced software design, particularly aspects relating to distributed systems and software architecture.

SE321 Software Quality Assurance and Testing

Broad coverage of software quality and testing.

SE322 Software Requirements Analysis

Broad coverage of software requirements, applied to a variety of types of software.

SE323 Software Project Management

In-depth course about project management. It is assumed that by the time students take this course, they will have a broad and deep understanding of other aspects of software engineering.

6.3.2 Core software engineering package II

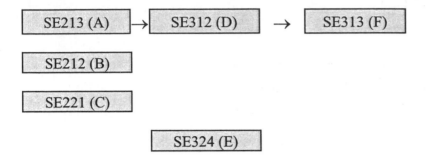

Note that SE212-hci has already been discussed in the context of package 1. The main differences between this package and package I are as follows:

- This package groups all of the formal methods material into a single course: SE313, introducing this material later in the program than package 1 does.

- The process, management, and quality material is packaged in different combinations.

- The design material is treated in a more top-down manner, starting with architectures first.

SE213 Design and Architecture of Large Software Systems

Modeling and design of large-scale, evolvable systems; managing and planning the development of such systems—including the discussion of configuration management and software architecture.

SE221 Software Testing

In-depth course on all aspects of testing, as well as other aspects of verification and validation, including specifying testable requirements, reviews, and product assurance.

SE312 Low-Level Design of Software

Techniques for low-level design and construction, including formal approaches. Detailed design for evolvability.

SE324 Software Process and Management

Software processes in general; requirements processes and management; evolution processes; quality processes; project personnel management; project planning.

SE313 Formal Methods in Software Engineering

Approaches to software design and construction that employ mathematics to achieve higher levels of quality. Mathematical foundations of formal methods; formal modeling; validation of formal models; formal design analysis; program transformations.

6.3.3 Software engineering capstone project

As discussed in the guidelines presented in the previous chapter, a capstone project course is essential in a software engineering degree program. The capstone course gives students the opportunity to undertake a significant software engineering project, in which they can deepen their knowledge of many SEEK areas. It should cover a full year (that is, 80 lecture-equivalent-hours). It covers a few hours of a variety of SEEK topics, because it is expected that students will learn some material on their own during this course, and will deepen students' knowledge in several areas to the "a" level of Bloom's taxonomy.

SE400

SE400 Software Engineering Capstone Project

Provides students, working in groups, with a significant project experience in which they can integrate much of the material they have learned in their program, including matters relating to requirements, design, human factors, professionalism, and project management.

6.4 Completing the curriculum: Additional courses

The introductory and core SE courses discussed in the last two sections cover much of the required material, but there are still several categories of courses remaining to discuss. Full details of new courses, including a formal calendar description, prerequisites, learning objectives, teaching modules, mapping to SEEK, and other material, is found in Appendix A. Appendix A also has a mapping to SEEK of courses borrowed from the CCCS volume.

6.4.1 Courses covering the remaining compulsory material

Intermediate fundamental computer science courses (Int)

The intermediate fundamental computer science courses are CCCS courses in the 200 series, and cover much of the remaining CMP.cf topics. Any curriculum covering SEEK will need at least two of these; the patterns in the next section all have three selected courses, but that illustrates only one possible approach. Some curricula, not shown here, might want to spread the intermediate SEEK CMP.cf material out over more than three courses.

Nontechnical (NT) compulsory courses

The nontechnical compulsory courses primarily cover the FND.ec topic and the PRF area of SEEK—that is, engineering economics, communication, and professionalism. Although it would be possible to compress the necessary SEEK material into a single course, we show the material spread over three courses so it can be covered in more depth.

NT272 Engineering Economics

This is a standard engineering economics course as taught in many universities. A relatively small fraction of this course is actually required by SEEK, but it would be desirable for software engineering students to learn more than that minimum.

NT181 Group Dynamics and Communication

Communication and writing skills are highly regarded in the software industry, but they are also fundamental to success in collegiate careers.

NT291 Professional Software Engineering Practice

Professional practice is concerned with the knowledge, skills, and attitudes that software engineers must possess to practice software engineering in a professional, responsible, and ethical manner. A suitable alternative course would be CS280 from the CCCS volume.

6.4.2 Non-SEEK courses

Certain curriculum slots in the patterns described below cover material outside SEEK's scope. We have included them to assist curriculum designers in developing programs that cover more than just SEEK. A certain number of such courses are essential for any interesting and well-rounded SE program. Curriculum designers and/or students have the flexibility to make their own choices based on their institutional or personal needs, or based on the needs of accreditation agencies that look for a broader engineering, science, or humanities background.

Mathematics courses that are not SE core

These cover two types of mathematics courses: material such as calculus that is not *essential* for a software engineering program according to SEEK, but is nonetheless required in many curricula for various reasons; and elective mathematics courses. We show sample course sequences containing such courses.

Most universities, especially in North America, often teach calculus in first year. SEEK does not contain calculus, because it is not used by software engineers except when doing domain-specific work (for example, for other engineers, for scientists, and for certain optimization tasks) and hence is not essential for *all* software engineering programs. However, there are a number of reasons why most programs include calculus:

- It is believed to help encourage abstract thinking and mathematical thinking in general.

- Many statistics courses have a calculus prerequisite.

- Although needed in the workplace by only a small percentage of software engineers, it is just not readily learned in the workplace.

Other mathematics areas commonly found in SE curricula are linear algebra and differential equations. See section 6.2.3 for math courses (discrete math and statistics) that are part of the SE core.

Technical elective (Tech elect) courses (SE/CS/IT/CE) that are not SE core

These courses cover technical material beyond the scope of the essential SEEK topics. Such courses could be compulsory in a particular program or electives chosen by students. They might cover topics in SEEK in greater depth than SEEK specifies, or they might cover material not listed in SEEK at all. This chapter does not give detailed specifications of such courses, but slots are shown in the course patterns. The reader can consult the Computer Science, Information Systems, or Computer Engineering volumes for examples.

Science/engineering courses covering non-SEEK topics

These cover material such as physics, chemistry, and electrical engineering. Most software engineering programs, especially in North America, will include some such courses, particularly physics courses.

The rationale for including science courses is that they give students experience with the scientific method and experimentation. Similarly, taking other engineering courses expands students' appreciation for engineering in general. Taking some science and engineering courses will also help students who later on want to develop software in those domains.

Courses in this category are not specified in this document in detail.

General nontechnical (Gen ed) courses

These slots are for courses in business, social sciences, humanities, arts, and so on. Most programs will make some such courses compulsory, particularly in the US, where there is a tradition of requiring some liberal arts. Some universities will want to incorporate specific streams of nontechnical courses (such as a stream of business courses).

6.5   Curriculum patterns

In this section we present some example patterns showing how the courses described in the last three sections can be arranged into a degree program along with additional noncore courses.

All of the patterns should be seen as examples; they are not intended to be prescriptive (unlike SEEK). They illustrate approaches to packaging SEEK topics in various contexts.

The main features that differentiate the patterns are:
- The international context
- The computer science or engineering school context
- Whether software engineering is to be taught starting in the first or second year

- Whether there are two semesters per academic year or three quarters

Pattern SE: Recommended General Structure

Year 1		Year 2		Year 3		Year 4	
Sem 1A	Sem 1B	Sem 2A	Sem 2B	Sem 3A	Sem 3B	Sem 4A	Sem 4B
Intro Computing Sequence			CS(Int)	CS(Int)	CS(Int)	SE400	SE400
CS105	CS106	*Calc 1*	*Calc 2*	MA271	SE	SE	*Tech elect*
NT		SE200/201	SE	SE	SE	*Tech elect*	*Tech elect*
		NT	SE	NT	*Tech elect*		

The remainder of the chapter is devoted to illustrating specific instances of applying Pattern SE in varying contexts.

Pattern N2S-1: North American Year-2-Start with Semesters

This pattern illustrates one way that courses can be arranged that should be widely adaptable to the needs of many North American universities operating on a semester system. Many course slots are left undefined to allow for adaptation. Two example adaptations are shown later.

The pattern starts its technical content with CS101, CS102, and CS103. The pattern also has SE201 taken in parallel with CS103 (see above for discussion of this sequence); SE101, SE102, CS103, SE200 sequence could be substituted. Following the introductory course SE201 (or SE200), students would take one of the packages of six SE courses described above that cover specific areas in depth.

There is considerable flexibility in the intermediate fundamental CS courses; a set of CCCS courses that cover appropriate areas of SEEK is suggested.

We have included three nontechnical courses to cover relevant areas of SEEK. We suggest starting with a communications course (such as NT181) very early, and deferring the ethics course (such as NT291), as shown, until students gain more maturity. Many variations are possible, however, including rolling the SEEK material in these courses into one or two courses instead of three.

We have shown the traditional Calculus 1 and Calculus 2 in first year, with the software engineering mathematics starting in second term of first year. From a pedagogical point of view, it could be argued that calculus should being delayed; however, teaching calculus in first year allows SE programs to mesh with existing CS and SE programs; it also ensures that SE students take calculus in classes with other students of the same age group.

Year1		Year 2		Year 3		Year 4	
Sem 1A	Sem 1B	Sem 2A	Sem 2B	Sem 3A	Sem 3B	Sem 4A	Sem 4B
CS101	CS102	CS103	CS (Int)	CS (Int)	CS(Int)	SE400	SE400
Calc 1	*Calc 2*	CS106	SE A	MA271	SE D	SE F	*Tech elect*
NT 181	CS105	SE201	SE212	SE C	SE E	*Tech elect*	*Tech elect*
--	--	NT 272	--	NT 291	*Tech elect*	--	--
--	--	--	--	--	--	--	--

Pattern N2S-1c - in a computer-science department

The pattern shown below is typical of a software engineering program that might be built in a computer science context. This is an adaptation of Pattern N2S-1, as shown above. Such programs may have evolved from computer science programs or can co-exist with computer science.

Year1		Year 2		Year 3		Year 4	
Sem 1A	Sem 1B	Sem 2A	Sem 2B	Sem 3A	Sem 3B	Sem 4A	Sem 4B
CS101	CS102	CS103	CS220	CS226	CS270T	SE400	SE400
Calc 1	*Calc 2*	CS106	SE A	MA271	SE D	SE F	*Tech elect*
NT181	CS105	SE201	SE212	SE C	SE E	*Tech elect*	*Tech elect*
Physics	*Any science*	NT272	*Linear Alg*	NT291	*Tech elect*	*Tech elect*	*Tech elect*
Gen ed	*Gen ed*	--	*Gen ed*	*Gen ed*	*Gen ed*	*Gen ed*	*Gen ed*

Pattern N2S-1e: in an engineering department

Programs in a North American engineering department typically begin with a rigorous calculus sequence (three semesters), probability and statistics, physics, and chemistry. Introductory courses in other areas of engineering are given during the first year. For SE programs in EE or CE departments, circuits and electricity are common. Programming for engineers is usually required in the first year. The introductory computer science sequence is often the compressed CS111, CS112 (CCCS) sequence, although we have maintained the three-course sequence below because we believe this is much better for software engineers.

Year1		Year 2		Year 3		Year 4	
Sem 1A	Sem 1B	Sem 2A	Sem 2B	Sem 3A	Sem 3B	Sem 4A	Sem 4B
CS101	CS102	CS103	CS220	CS226	CS270T	SE400	SE400
Calc 1	*Calc 2*	CS106	SE A	MA271	SE D	SE F	*Tech elect*
NT181	CS105	SE201	SE212	SE C	SE E	*Tech elect*	*Tech elect*
Physics 1	*Physics 2*	NT272	*Lin Alg*	NT291	*Tech elect*	*Tech elect*	*Tech elect*
Chemistry	*Engineering*	*Calc 3*	*Gen ed*	*Gen ed*	*Gen ed*	*Gen ed*	*Gen ed*

Pattern E-1: Compressed model for a country in which it is assumed calculus and science is not needed or is taught in high school, and less general education is needed

Some countries, including most of the UK, have secondary school systems that bring students to a higher level of science and mathematics. Such systems also tend to have very focused postsecondary education, requiring much less in the way of general education (humanities and so on). The following pattern shows one way of teaching SE in those environments.

Year1		Year 2		Year 3	
Term 1A	Term 1B	Term 2A	Term 2B	Term 3A	Term 3B
CS101	CS102	CS103	CS merged	SE400	SE400
CS105	CS106	MA271	SE D	SE F	Tech elect
NT181	SE201	SE A	SE E	Tech elect	Tech elect
NT272	NT291	SE C	SE212	Tech elect	Tech elect
--	--	--	--	--	--

Pattern E-2: Another model for a country in which calculus and science is not needed.

This pattern also illustrates the use of SE101 and SE102, as well as the delay of some of the core SE courses until students have gained maturity.

Year1		Year 2		Year 3		Year 4	
Sem 1A	Sem 1B	Sem 2A	Sem 2B	Sem 3A	Sem 3B	Sem 4A	Sem 4B
SE101	SE102	CS103	SE200	SE A	SE212	SE D	SE F
CS overview	CS106	CS220	CS226	Tech elect	SE C	SE E	SE400
CS105	MA271	NT291	CS270T	Tech elect	Tech elect	SE400	Tech elect
NT181	NT272	--	--	--	--	--	--
--	--	--	--	--	--	--	--

Pattern N3Q-1: North American year 3 start—Quartered

Some North American universities operate on a quarter system, with three quarters instead of two semesters. The following pattern accommodates this, assuming that four courses are taught each quarter. This pattern also illustrates one way of delaying the SE core courses until third year.

Year 1			Year 2		
Quarter 1A	Quarter 1B	Quarter 1C	Quarter 2A	Quarter 2B	Quarter 2C
CS101	Calc 2	CS102	CS 103	CS270T	CS226
Calc 1	Chemistry	Calc 3	CS220	CS106	Math
Physics 1	Physics 2	Engineering	CS105	NT291	Gen ed
Gen ed	NT181	Gen ed	Math	--	--

Year 3			Year 4		
Quarter 3A	Quarter 3B	Quarter 3C	Quarter 4A	Quarter 4B	Quarter 4C
SE201	SE A	SE D	SE400	SE400	SE400
SE212	SE C	SE E	SE F	Tech elect	Tech elect
MA271	Tech elect	Gen ed	Tech elect	Gen ed	Gen ed
NT272	--	--	Gen ed	--	--

Pattern N1S: US model showing starting SE early in CS courses

This model shows the use of the first-year-start sequence: SE101, SE102, and SE200.

Year1		Year 2		Year 3		Year 4	
Sem 1A	Sem 1B	Sem 2A	Sem 2B	Sem 3A	Sem 3B	Sem 4A	Sem 4B
SE101	SE102	CS103	CS270	CS220	SE D	CS226	SE400
Calc 1	Calc 2	SE200	SE212	SE A	SE E	SE400	Tech elect
CS105	CS106	Physics 1	MA271	SE C	Tech elect	SE F	Tech elect
Gen ed	Psychology	NT181	Physics 2	Sci Elect	NT291	Gen ed	Gen ed
Gen ed	Gen ed	Gen ed	Sci Elect	Sci Elect	--	NT272	--

Pattern Jpn 1: Japanese pattern 1

This pattern shows how the courses could be taught in Japan. This is based on a model produced by the Information Processing Society of Japan (IPSJ). The IPSJ curriculum has been adapted slightly to include the courses in this document. Some of the distinguishing features are: no calculus or science electives, a large number of prescribed computer science courses, general education mostly in the first year, and extra programming courses in the first year. The IPSJ program has a variable numbers of hours for the courses. To simplify, we have shown a program where courses have a standard number of hours.

Year 1		Year 2		Year 3		Year 4	
Sem 1A	Sem 1B	Sem 2A	Sem 2B	Sem 3A	Sem 3B	Sem 4A	Sem 4B
Calc 1	Calc 2	CS	CS	CS	CS	SE400	SE400
CS111	CS112	CS	CS	SE C	SE E	Tech elect	NT181
CS extra	CS extra	CS	CS	SE D	SE F	Tech elect	Tech elect
CS105	CS106	CS	CS	NT291	NT272	--	--
Gen ed	Gen ed	MA271	SE A	SysApp Spec	SysApp Spec	--	--
Gen ed	Gen ed	SE201	SE212	SysApp Spec	SysApp Spec	--	--

Pattern Aus1: Australian model with four courses per semester

This pattern shows a pattern that might be suitable in Australia. It has been adapted from the curriculum of an Australian university. Many universities in Australia are moving towards having only four courses per semester, with students consequently learning more per course than if they were taking five or six courses. As a result, the 40-hour courses discussed in this document don't fit and would have to be adapted.

Some of the adaptations are:

- The essentials of NT181 and NT272 are covered in a single somewhat longer course.

- The discrete math material is combined into a single somewhat longer course.

- The six-course software engineering sequences are not used. Instead there are five compulsory SE courses beyond SE201. Two of these courses are project courses, allowing for learning using a nonlecture format.

- Material from SE323 and NT291 are taught in the same course.

- Some of the SE courses broadly introduce SEEK topics, with depth being achieved by choosing from particular sets of technical electives.

Year1		Year 2		Year 3		Year 4	
Sem 1A	Sem 1B	Sem 2A	Sem 2B	Sem 3A	Sem 3B	Sem 4A	Sem 4B
CS101	CS102	CS220	CS103	CS	Team proj	SE400	SE400
Calc 1	Lin. Alg	CS270T	SE	SE	Tech elect	SE323 NT291	Tech elect
NT181/ NT 272	Dig Logic	SE201	Team proj	Tech elect	Tech elect	Tech elect	--
Intro EE	CS105 CS 106	MA271	--	--	--	--	--

Pattern Isr 1: Model for Israel

This pattern is derived from an Israeli university's computer science program. The program has a large number of prescribed computer science courses. To make an SE program, we have replaced some of these with SE courses.

Year1		Year 2		Year 3		Year 4	
Sem 1A	Sem 1B	Sem 2A	Sem 2B	Sem 3A	Sem 3B	Sem 4A	Sem 4B
CS101	CS102	CS103	CS	SE A	SE D	SE400	SE400
Dig sys	CS	CS	CS	SE212	SE E	SE F	--
Calc 1	Calc 2	CS	CS	SE C	NT291	NT272	--
Lin. Alg	Abst Alg	MA271	CS	CS	--	--	--
NT181	Combinatorics	CS105 CS106	CS	CS	--	--	--

Chapter 7: Adaptation to Alternative Environments

Software engineering curricula do not exist in isolation. They are found in institutions; and these institutions have differing environments, goals, and practices. Software engineering curricula must be able to be delivered in a variety of fashions and to be part of many different types of institutions.

There are two main categories of "alternative" environments that will be discussed in this section. The first is the alternative teaching environment. These environments use nonstandard delivery methods. The second is the alternative institutional *environment*. These institutions differ in some significant fashion from the usual university.

7.1   Alternative teaching environments

As higher education has become more universal, the standard teaching environment has tended toward an instructor in the front of a classroom. Although some institutions still retain limited aspects of a tutor-student relationship, the dominant delivery method in most higher education today is classroom-type instruction. The instructor presents material to a class using lecture or lecture/discussion presentation techniques. The lectures can be augmented by appropriate laboratory work. Class sizes range from fewer than 10 to more than 500.

Instruction in the computing disciplines has been notable because of the large amount of experimentation with delivery methods. This might be the result of the instructors' familiarity with technology's capabilities. It might also be the result of the youthfulness of the computing disciplines. Regardless of the cause, there are numerous papers in the *SIGCSE Bulletin*, in the proceedings of the Conference on Software Engineering Education & Training (CSEE&T) conferences, in the proceeding of the Frontiers in Education (FIE) conferences, and in similar forums that recount significant modifications to the conventional lecture and lecture/discussion-based classrooms. Examples include all-laboratory instruction, the use of electronic whiteboards and tablet computers, problem-based learning, role-playing, activity-based learning, and various studio approaches that integrate laboratory, lecture, and discussion. As the report has mentioned elsewhere, it is imperative that experimentation and exploration be part of any software engineering curriculum. Necessary curriculum changes are difficult to implement in an environment that does not support experimentation and exploration. A software engineering curriculum will rapidly become out of date unless there is a conscious effort to implement regular change.

Much recent curricular experimentation has focused on distance learning. The term is not well defined. It applies to situations in which students are in different physical locations during a scheduled class. It also applies to situations where students are in different physical locations and there is no scheduled class time. It is important to distinguish between these two cases. It is also important to recognize other cases, such as situations in which students cannot attend regularly scheduled classes.

7.1.1 Students at different physical locations

Instructing students at different physical locations is a problem with several solutions. Audio and video links have been used for many years, and broadband Internet connections are less costly and more accessible. Instructor-student interaction is possible after all involved have learned how to manage the technology without confusion. Two-way video makes such interaction almost as natural as the interaction in a self-contained classroom. Online databases of problems and examples can be used to further support this type of instruction. Web resources, e-mail, and Internet chat can provide a reasonable instructor "office hour" experience. Assignments can be submitted by e-mail or through a direct Internet connection. The current computing literature and departmental Web sites contain numerous descriptions of distance learning techniques.

It should be noted that a complete solution to the problem of delivering courses to students in different locations is not a trivial matter and any solution will require significant planning and appropriate additional support. Some might argue that there is no need to make special provision for added time and support costs when one merely increases the size of an existing class by adding some distance students. Experience indicates that this is always a very poor idea.

Students in software engineering programs need to experience working in teams. Students who are geographically isolated need to be accommodated in some fashion. It is unreasonable to expect that a geographically separated team will be able to do all of its work using e-mail, chat, blogs, and newsgroups. Geographically separated teams need additional monitoring and support. Videoconferencing and teleconferencing should be considered. Instructors might also want to schedule some meetings with the teams, if distances make this feasible. Beginning students require significantly more monitoring than advanced students because of their lack of experience with geographically separated teams.

One other problem with geographically diverse students is the evaluation of student performance. Appropriate responsible parties will need to be found to proctor examinations and check identities of examinees. Care should be taken to insure that evaluation of student performance is done in a variety of ways. Placing too much reliance on one method (for example, written examinations) can make the evaluations unreliable.

7.1.2 Students in class at different times

Some institutions have a history of providing instruction to mature students who have full-time jobs. Because of their work obligations, employed students are often unable to attend regular class meetings. Videotaped lectures, copies of class notes, and electronic copies of class presentations are all useful tools in this situation. A course Web site, a class newsgroup, and a class distribution list can provide further support.

There is also instruction that does not have any scheduled class meetings. Self-scheduled and self-paced classes have been used at many institutions. Classes have also been designed to be completely Web-based. Commercial and open-source software has been developed to support many aspects of self-paced and Web-based courses. Experience shows that the development of self-paced and Web-based instructional materials is very expensive and time consuming.

Students who do not have scheduled classroom instruction will still need team activities and experiences. Many of the comments made above about geographically diverse teams will also apply to them. An additional problem is created when students are learning at wildly different rates. Because different students will cover content at different times, it is not feasible to have content instruction and projects integrated in the same unit. Self-paced project courses are another serious problem. It will be difficult to coordinate team activities when different team members are working at different paces.

7.2   Curricula for alternative institutional environments

7.2.1   Articulation problems

Articulation problems arise when students have taken one set of courses at one institution or in one program and need to apply them to meet the requirements of a different institution and/or program.

If software engineering curricula existed in isolation, there would be no articulation problems. But this is rarely the case. Software engineering programs exist in universities with multiple colleges, schools, divisions, departments, and programs. Software engineering programs exist in universities that cooperate and compete with other universities and institutions. Some secondary schools offer university-level instruction, and students expect to receive appropriate credit and placement. Satisfactory completion of a curriculum must be certified when the student has taken classes in different areas of the university as well as at other institutions. Software engineering programs must be designed and managed so that articulation problems are minimized. This means that the institution's internal and external environments must be considered when designing a curriculum.

7.2.2   Coordination with other university curricula

Many of the core classes in a software engineering curriculum could also be core classes in another curriculum. An introductory computer science course could be required for the curricula in computer science, computer engineering, and software engineering. Certain architecture courses might be part of curricula in computer science, computer engineering, software engineering, and electrical engineering. Mathematics courses could be required for curricula in mathematics, computer science, software engineering, and computer engineering. A project management course might be required by software engineering and management information systems. Upper-level software engineering courses could be taken as part of computer science or computer engineering programs. In most universities, there will be pressure to have courses do double duty whenever possible.

Courses that are a part of more than one curriculum must be carefully designed. There is great pressure to include everything of significance to all of the relevant disciplines. This pressure must be resisted. It is impossible to satisfy everyone's desires. Courses that serve two masters will inevitably have to omit topics that would be present were it not for the other master. Curriculum implementers must recognize that perfection is impossible and impractical. The minor content loss when courses are designed to be part of several curricula is more that compensated for by the experience of interacting with students with other ideas and background.

Indeed, a case can be made that such experiences are so important in a software engineering curriculum that special efforts should be made to create courses common to several curricula.

7.2.3 Cooperation with other institutions

In today's world, students complete their university education via a variety of pathways. Although many students attend just one institution, a substantial number attend more than one. For a wide variety of reasons, many students begin their baccalaureate degree program at one institution and complete it at another. In so doing, students might change their career goals or declared majors, move from a liberal arts program to an engineering or scientific program, satisfy interim program requirements at one institution, engage in work-related experiences, or be coping with financial, geographic, or personal constraints.

Software engineering curricula must be designed so these students can complete the program without undue delay and repetition, through recognition of comparable coursework and aligned programs. It is straightforward to grant credit for previous work (whether in another department, school, college, or university) when the content of the courses being compared is substantially identical. There are problems, however, when the content is not substantially similar. No one wants a student to receive double credit for learning the same thing twice. By the same token, no one wants a student to repeat a whole course merely because a limited amount of content topic was not covered in the other course. Faculty do not want to see a student's progress unduly delayed because of articulation issues; therefore, the wisest criteria to use when determining transfer and placement credit are whether the student can reasonably be expected to address any content deficiencies in a timely fashion and succeed in subsequent courses.

To the extent that course equivalencies can be identified and addressed in advance via an articulation agreement, student interests will best be served. Many institutions have formal articulation agreements with those institutions from which they routinely receive transfer students. For example, such agreements are frequently found in the United States between baccalaureate-degree granting institutions and the associate-degree granting institutions that send them transfer students. Other examples can be seen in the 3-2 agreements in the United States between liberal arts and engineering institutions. These agreements allow a student to take three years at a liberal arts institution and two years at an engineering institution, receiving a bachelor of arts degree and a bachelor of science degree.

When formulating articulation agreements and designing curricula, it is important to consider any existing accreditation requirements. An accredited program can only retain accreditation for all of its students if it can show that students entering from other institutions have learned substantially similar material.

The European Credit Transfer System is another attempt to reduce articulation problems in that continent.

7.3 Programs for associate-degree-granting institutions in the United States and community colleges in Canada

In the United States, as many as one-half of baccalaureate graduates initiated their studies in associate-degree granting institutions. For this reason, it is important to outline a software engineering program of study that can be initiated in the two-year college setting and is specifically designed for seamless transfer into an upper-division (years 3 and 4) program. Regardless of their skills upon entry into the two-year college, students must complete the coursework in its entirety to well-defined competency points to ensure success in the subsequent software engineering coursework at the baccalaureate level. For some students, this might require more than two years of study at the associate level. Regardless, the goal is the same: to provide a program of study that prepares the student for the upper-level institution.

Following is a recommended software engineering program of study for implementation by associate-degree granting institutions. Students who complete this program could reasonably expect to transfer into the upper-division program at the baccalaureate institution. Although designed with the United States in mind, certain colleges in Canada and other countries might be able to adopt a similar approach.

Proposed software engineering technical core for North American community colleges

For descriptions of the computing and mathematics courses listed below, see the report titled *Computing Curricula 2003: Guidelines for Associate-Degree Curricula in Computer Science* [ACM 2002].

Computing courses
The three-course sequence
CS101i – Programming Fundamentals
CS102i – The Object-Oriented Paradigm
CS103i – Data Structures and Algorithms
or the three-course sequence
CS101o – Introduction to Object-Oriented Programming
CS102o – Objects and Data Abstraction
CS103o – Algorithms and Data Structures

SE201-int – Introduction to Software Engineering for Software Engineers
Institutions can also elect to create a software engineering curriculum based on the SE-specific courses (SE101, SE102, CS103, SE200) outlined in chapter 6 of this report.

Mathematics courses
CS105 – Discrete Structures I
CS106 – Discrete Structures II

The following are for articulation with typical university requirements, and do not cover core SEEK material
Calculus I
Calculus II

See also the baccalaureate institution for requirements; some institutions may require linear algebra or differential equations.

<u>Laboratory science courses</u>
Two courses in lab science for articulation with most baccalaureate programs. Recommended: two physics courses or one physics plus one chemistry course.

<u>General education</u>
Students also complete first- and second-year general education requirements, along with software engineering technical core.

7.3.1 Special programs

Because software engineering is such a new discipline, there is a significant demand for certain types of special programs. Some people want to retrain in a new field. Others already have a degree in a related field and want a postgraduate diploma in software engineering. The curricula for such programs must take into account students' previous education as well as their career goals.

It would be foolish to attempt to cram a whole undergraduate curriculum in software engineering into a short retraining program or a one-year postgraduate program. Such an effort does not serve the needs of these students. These programs are best when they have appropriate entrance standards that require at least some practical experience. When this is the case, the students are usually highly motivated. Such students can have their experience serve as a reasonable substitute for some of the content that would normally be a part of an undergraduate curriculum.

Chapter 8:   Program Implementation and Assessment

8.1   Curriculum resources and infrastructure

Once a curriculum is established, an educational program's success critically depends on three specific elements: the faculty, the student body, and the infrastructure. Furthermore, it is also very important to have continuous industry involvement from the outset.

8.1.1   Faculty

A high-quality faculty and staff is perhaps the single most critical element in a program's success. There must be sufficient faculty to teach the program's courses and support the educational activities needed to deliver a curriculum and reach the program's objectives; the teaching and administrative load must allow time for faculty to engage in scholarly and professional activities. This is critical given the dynamic nature of computing and software engineering.

A software engineering program needs faculty who possess both advanced education in computing with a focus on software, and sufficient experience in software engineering practice. However, because of the relative youth of software engineering, recruiting faculty with the attributes of traditional faculty (academic credentials, effective teaching capabilities, and research potential) plus software engineering professional experience is particularly challenging [Glass 2003]. For example, only recently have PhD programs in software engineering been established in the US [ISRI 2003]. Software engineering faculty should be encouraged and supported in their efforts to become and remain current in industrial software engineering practice through applied research, industry internships, consulting, and so on.

8.1.2   Students

Another critical factor in a program's success is the quality of its student body. There should be admission standards that help assure that students are properly prepared for the program. Procedures and processes are needed that track and document students' progress through the program to ensure that graduates meet the program objectives and desired outcomes. Appropriate metrics, consistent with the institutional mission and program objectives, must exist to guide students toward completion of the program in a reasonable period of time, and to measure the success of the graduates in meeting the program objectives.

Interaction with students about curriculum development and delivery provides valuable information for assessing and analyzing a curriculum. Involvement of students in professional organizations and activities extends and enhances their education.

8.1.3   Infrastructure

The program must provide adequate infrastructure and technical support. This includes well-equipped laboratories and classrooms, adequate study areas, and technically competent laboratory staff to provide adequate technical support. For student project teams to be effective, adequate facilities are also needed to carry out team activities such as team meetings, inspections and walkthroughs, customer reviews, assessment, and reports on team progress. There should also be sufficient reference and documentation material and a library with sufficient holdings in software engineering literature and across related computing disciplines.

Maintaining laboratories and a modern suite of applicable software tools can be a daunting task because of the dynamic, accelerating pace of advances in software and hardware technology. However, as pointed out earlier in this document, it is essential that "students gain experience using appropriate and up-to-date tools."

An academic program in software engineering must have sufficient leadership and staff to provide proper program administration. This should include adequate levels of student advising, support services, and interaction with relevant constituencies such as employers and alumni. The advisory function of the faculty must be recognized by the institution and must be given appropriate administrative support.

There must be sufficient financial resources to support the recruitment, development, and retention of adequate faculty and staff, the maintenance of an appropriate infrastructure, and all necessary program activities.

8.1.4   Industry participation

An additional critical element in the success of a software engineering program is the involvement and active participation of industry. Industrial advisory boards and industry-academic partnerships help maintain curriculum relevance and currency. Such relations can support a variety of activities including programmatic advice from an industry perspective, student and faculty industrial internships, integration of industry projects into the curriculum, industry guest lectures, and visiting faculty positions from industry.

8.2   Assessment and accreditation issues

To maintain a quality curriculum, a software engineering program should be assessed on a regular basis. Many feel assessment is best accomplished in conjunction with a recognized accreditation organization. Curriculum guidance and accreditation standards and criteria are provided by a number of accreditation organizations across a variety of nations and regions [ABET 2000, BCS 2001,CEAB 2002, ECSA 2000, King 1997, IEI 2000, ISA 1999, JABEE 2003]. In other countries, assessment is carried out by the government under a standard predefined curriculum model or set of curriculum standards and guidelines. In 1998, a joint IEEE/ACM task force drafted accreditation criteria for software engineering [Barnes 1998], which included guidance and requirements in the following areas: faculty, curriculum, laboratory and computing resources, students, institutional support, and assessment of program effectiveness. In terms of curriculum, it stipulates that the bachelor's program in software engineering must include approximately equal segments in *software engineering*, in *computer science and engineering*, in appropriate *supporting areas*, and in *advanced* materials.

Accreditation typically includes periodic external review of programs, which assures that programs meet a minimum set of criteria and adhere to an accreditation organization's standards. A popular approach to assessment and accreditation is an outcomes-based approach for which educational objectives and/or student outcomes are established first, and then the curriculum, an administrative organization, and the infrastructure needed to meet the objectives and outcomes is put into place.

The assessment should evaluate the program objectives and desired outcomes, the curriculum content, and the delivery, and serve as the primary feedback mechanism for continuous improvement.

In addition to this document and the previous cited accreditation organizations, there are many sources for assisting a program in forming and assessing its objectives and outcomes [Bagert 1999, Lethbridge 2000, Meyer 2001, Naveda 1997, Parnas 1999, Saiedian 2002, IWCSEA].

8.3   SE in other computing-related disciplines

Software engineering does not, of course, exist by itself. It has strong association to other areas of science and technology, especially those related to computing. At one end we have the work of scientists, and at the other end we have technology and technical specialists. Toward the center of the spectrum is design, a distinctive feature of engineering programs.

Within this context, computer scientists are primarily focused on seeking new knowledge as, for example, in the form of new algorithms and data structures, new database information-retrieval methods, discovery of advanced graphics and human–computer interaction organizing principles, optimized operating systems and networks, and modern programming languages and tools that can be used to better the job of a software engineer (and computer engineer for that matter). It is of note that the CCCS volume has a chapter devoted to "Changes in the Computer Science Discipline," and there are a variety of views about computer science as a discipline. It is also worth mentioning that there is a need to distinguish computer science as it exists today, from what it may become in the near future as a discipline that studies the theoretical underpinnings and limitations of computing. David Parnas [Parnas 99] speaks to this issue in the statement "an engineer cannot be sure that a product is *fit-for-use* unless those limitations are known and have been taken into consideration." Such limitations include technological limitations (hardware and programming and design tools available) as well as the fundamental limitations (computability and complexity theory, and in particular information theory including noise and data corrections).

Information technology and other more applied and specialized programs, such as network and system administration, and all engineering technology programs, fit at the opposite end of the spectrum from computer science. Software engineering and computer engineering fall in the center of the spectrum with their focus on engineering design. The central role that engineering design plays in software engineering is discussed elsewhere in this document. The software engineer's focus should be on understanding on how to use the theory to solve practical problems.

Because of the pervasive nature of software, the scope for the types of problems in software engineering might be significantly wider than that of other branches of engineering. Within a specific *domain of application*, the designer relies on specific education and experience to evaluate many possible solutions. They have to determine which standard parts can be used and which parts have to be developed from scratch. To make the necessary decisions, the designer must have a fundamental knowledge of specialty subjects. While domains span the entire spectrum of industry, government, and society, there is a shorter list of concrete specialty application areas such as scientific information systems, including bioinformatics, astroinformatics, ecoinformatics, microsystems, aeronautics, and astronautics.

Bibliography for Software Engineering Education

[Abelson 1985] H. Abelson and G.J. Sussman, *Structure and Interpretation of Computer Programs*, MIT Press, 1985.

[ABET 2000] Accreditation Board for Engineering and Technology, *Accreditation Policy and Procedure Manual*, ABET, Nov. 2000; http://www.abet.org/images/policies.pdf.

[ACM 1965] ACM Curriculum Committee on Computer Science, "An Undergraduate Program in Computer Science—Preliminary Recommendations," *Comm. ACM*, Sept. 1965.

[ACM 1968] ACM Curriculum Committee on Computer Science, "Curriculum '68: Recommendations for the Undergraduate Program in Computer Science," *Comm. ACM*, Mar. 1968.

[ACM 1978] ACM Curriculum Committee on Computer Science, "Curriculum '78: Recommendations for the Undergraduate Program in Computer Science," *Comm. ACM*, Mar. 1979.

[ACM 1989] ACM Task Force on the Core of Computer Science, "Computing as a Discipline," *Comm. ACM*, Jan. 1989.

[ACM 1998] ACM/IEEE-CS Joint Task Force on Software Engineering Ethics and Professional Practices, *Software Engineering Code of Ethics and Professional Practice*, Version 5.2, http://www.acm.org/serving/se/code.htm, Sept. 1998.

[ACM 1999] *ACM Two-Year College Education Committee. Guidelines for Associate-Degree and Certificate Programs to Support Computing in a Networked Environment*, Assoc. for Computing Machinery, Sept. 1999.

[ACM 2002] ACM/IEEE-Curriculum 2001 Task Force, *Computing Curricula 2003: Guidelines for Associate-Degree Curricula in Computer Science*, Dec. 2002; http://www.acmtyc.org/reports/TYC_CS2003_report.pdf.

[Andrews 2000] J.H. Andrews and H.L. Lutfiyya, "Experiences with a Software Maintenance Project Course," *IEEE Trans. Education*, Nov. 2000.

[APP 2000] Advanced Placement Program, *Introduction of Java in 2003-2004*, The College Board, Dec. 2000; http://www.collegeboard.org/ap/computer-science.

[Bagert 1999] D. Bagert et al., *Guidelines for Software Engineering Education*, Version 1.0, CMU/SEI-99-TR-032, Software Eng. Inst., Carnegie Mellon Univ., 1999.

[Barnes 1998] B. Barnes et al., "Draft Software Engineering Accreditation Criteria," *Computer*, Apr. 1998.

[Barta 1993] B.Z. Barta, S.L. Hung, and K.R. Cox, eds., IFIP Transactions A40, Software Engineering Education, *Proc. IFIP W.G. 3.4/SRIG-ET (SEARCC) Int'l Working Conf.*, North-Holland, 1993.

[Bauer 1972] F.L. Bauer, "Software Engineering," *Information Processing*, 71, 1972.

[BCS 1989a] British Computer Society and the Institution of Electrical Engineers, *Undergraduate Curricula for Software Engineers*, London, June 1989.

[BCS 1989b] British Computer Society and the Institution of Electrical Engineers, *Software in Safety-Related Systems*, London, Oct. 1989.

[BCS 2001] British Computer Society, *Guidelines on Course Exemption & Accreditation for Information for Universities and Colleges*, Aug. 2001; http://www1.bcs.org.uk/link.asp?sectionID=1114.

[Beidler et al, 1985] J. Beidler, R. Austing, and L. Cassel, "Computing Programs in Small Colleges," *Comm. ACM,* June 1985.

[Bennett 1986] W. Bennett, "A Position Paper on Guidelines for Electrical and Computer Engineering Education," *IEEE Trans. Education*, Aug. 1986.

[Bloom 1956] B.S. Bloom, ed., *Taxonomy of Educational Objectives: The Classification of Educational Goals: Handbook I, Cognitive Domain*, Longmans, 1956.

[Bourque 2001] P. Bourque and R. Dupuis, eds. *Guide to the Software Engineering Body of Knowledge*, IEEE CS Press, 2001.

[Borstler 2002] J. Borstler et al., "Teaching PSP: Challenges and Lessons Learned," *IEEE Software*, Sept./Oct. 2002.

[Bott 1995] F. Bott et al., "Professional Issues in Software Engineering," 2nd ed., UCL Press, 1995.

[Brooks 95] F.P. Brooks, *The Mythical Man-Month, Essays on Software Engineering, Anniversary Edition*, Addison-Wesley, 1995.

[Budgen 2003] D. Budgen and J.E. Tomayko, "Norm Gibbs and His Contribution to Software Engineering Education through the SEI Curriculum Modules," *Proc. 16th Conf. CSEE&T*, Mar. 2003.

[Burnell 2002] L.J. Burnell, J.W. Priest, and J.R. Durrett, "Teaching Distributed Multidisciplinary Software Development," *IEEE Software*, Sept./Oct. 2002.

[Buxton 1970] J.N. Buxton, J.N. and B. Randell, eds., *Software Engineering Techniques*, Report of a Conference Sponsored by NATO Science Committee (Rome, 27 31 October, 1969), 1970.

[Carnegie 1992] Carnegie Commission on Science, Technology, and Government, *Enabling the Future: Linking Science and Technology to Societal Goals,* Carnegie Commission, Sept. 1992.

[Cheston 2002] G.A. Cheston and J.-P. Tremblay, "Integrating Software Engineering in Introductory Computing Courses," *IEEE Software*, Sept./Oct. 2002.

[CEAB 2002] Canadian Engineering Accreditation Board, *Accreditation Criteria and Procedures*, Canadian Council of Professional Engineers, 2002; http://www.ccpe.ca/e/files/report_ceab.pdf .

[COSINE 1967] COSINE Committee, *Computer Science in Electrical Engineering,* Commission on Engineering Education, Sept. 1967.

[Cowling 1998] A. Cowling, "The First Decade of an Undergraduate Degree Programme in Software Engineering," *Annals of Software Eng.*, vol. 6, 1998, pp. 61-90.

[CSAB 1986] Computing Sciences Accreditation Board, *Defining the Computing Sciences Professions*, Oct. 1986; http://www.csab.org/comp_sci_profession.html.

[CSAB 2000] Computing Sciences Accreditation Board, *Criteria for Accrediting Programs in Computer Science in the United States*, Version 1.0, Jan. 2000; http://www.csab.org/criteria2k_v10.html.

[CSTB 1994] Computing Science and Telecommunications Board, *Realizing the Information Future*, Nat'l Academy Press, 1994.

[CSTB 1999] Computing Science and Telecommunications Board, *Being Fluent with Information Technology*, Nat'l Academy Press, 1999.

[Curtis 1983] K.K. Curtis, *Computer Manpower: Is There a Crisis?* Nat'l Science Foundation, 1983; http://www.acm.org/sigcse/papers/curtis83/.

[Cybulski 2000] J.L. Cybulski and T. Linden, "Learning Systems Design with UML and Patterns," *IEEE Trans. Education*, Nov. 2000

[Davis 1997] G.B. Davis et al., *IS'97 Model Curriculum and Guidelines for Undergraduate Degree Programs in Information Systems*, Assoc. of Information Technology Professionals, 1997; http://webfoot.csom.umn.edu/faculty/gdavis/curcomre.pdf.

[Denning 1989] P.J. Denning et al., "Computing as a Discipline," *Comm. ACM*, Jan. 1989.

[Denning 1992] P.J. Denning, "Educating a New Engineer," *Comm. ACM*, Dec. 1992.

[Denning 1998] P.J. Denning, "Computing the Profession," *Educom Rev.*, Nov. 1998.

[Denning 1999] P.J. Denning, "Our Seed Corn is Growing in the Commons," *Information Impacts Magazine*, Mar. 1999; http://www.cisp.org/imp/march_99/denning/03_99denning.htm.

[EAB 1983] Educational Activities Board, *The 1983 Model Program in Computer Science and Engineering,* Tech. Report 932, IEEE Computer Soc., Dec. 1983.

[EAB 1986] Educational Activities Board, *Design Education in Computer Science and Engineering*, Tech. Report 971, IEEE Computer Soc., Oct. 1986.

[EC 1977] Education Committee of the IEEE Computer Soc., *A Curriculum in Computer Science and Engineering*, publication EHO119-8, IEEE Computer Soc., Jan. 1977.

[ECSA 2000] Eng. Council of South Africa, *Policy on Accreditation of University Bachelors Degrees*, Aug. 2000; http://www.ecsa.co.za/.

[Fairley 1985] R. Fairley, *Software Engineering Concepts*, McGraw-Hill, 1985.

[Finkelstein 1993] A. Finkelstein, "European Computing Curricula: A Guide and Comparative Analysis," *Computer J.*, vol. 36, no. 4, 1993, pp. 299-319.

[Fleddermann 2000] C.B. Fleddermann, "Engineering Ethics Cases for Electrical and Computer Engineering Students," *IEEE Trans. Education*, vol. 43, no. 3, Aug. 2000, pp. 284-287.

[Ford 1994] G. Ford, *A Progress Report on Undergraduate Software Engineering Education*, CMU/SEI-94-TR-11, Software Eng. Inst., Carnegie Mellon Univ., May 1994.

[Ford 1996] G. Ford and N.E. Gibbs, *A Mature Profession of Software Engineering*, CMU/SEI-96-TR-004, Software Eng. Inst., Carnegie Mellon Univ., Jan. 1996.

[Freeman 1976] P. Freeman, A.I. Wasserman, and R.E. Fairley, "Essential Elements of Software Engineering Education," *Proc. 2nd Int'l Conf. Software Eng.*, IEEE Computer Soc. Press, 1976, pp. 116-122.

[Freeman 1978] P. Freeman and A.I. Wasserman, "A Proposed Curriculum for Software Engineering Education," *Proc. 3rd Int'l Conf. Software Eng.*, IEEE Computer Soc. Press, 1978, pp. 56-62.

[Gibbs 1986] N.E. Gibbs and A.B. Tucker, "Model Curriculum for a Liberal Arts Degree in Computer Science," *Comm. ACM*, vol. 29, no. 3, Mar. 1986, pp. 202-210.

[Giladi 1999] R. Giladi, "An Undergraduate Degree Program for Communications Systems Engineering," *IEEE Trans. Education*, vol. 42, no. 4, Nov. 1999, pp. 295-304.

[Glass 2003] R.L. Glass, "A Big Problem in Academic Software Engineering and a Potential Outside-the-Box Solution," *IEEE Software*, vol. 20, no. 4, July/Aug. 2003.

[Gorgone 2002] J.T. Gorgone et al., *IS 2002: Model Curriculum for Undergraduate Degree Programs in Information Systems*, ACM, 2002.

[Hilburn 2002a] T.B. Hilburn, "Software Engineering Education: A Modest Proposal," *IEEE Software*, vol. 14, no. 4, Nov. 1997.

[Hilburn, 2002b] T.B. Hilburn and W.S. Humphrey, "The Impending Changes in Software Education," *IEEE Software*, vol. 19, no. 5, Sept./Oct. 2002, pp. 22-24.

[Hilburn, 2003] T.B. Hilburn, A.E.K. Sobel, G.W. Hislop, and R. Duley, "Engineering an Introductory Software Engineering Curriculum," *Proc. 16th Conf. CSEE&T*, Mar. 2003, pp. 99-106.

[Hunter 2001] R. Hunter and R.H. Thayer, eds., *Software Process Improvement,* IEEE Computer Soc., 2001.

[IEI 2000] The Institution of Engineers of Ireland, *Accreditation of Engineering Degrees*, May 2000, http://www.iei.ie/Accred/accofeng.pdf.

[ISA 1999] Institution of Engineers, Australia, *Manual for the Accreditation of Professional Engineering Programs*, Oct. 1999; http://www.ieaust.org.au/membership/res/downloads/AccredManual.pdf.

[ISRI 2003] Inst. for Software Research, Int'l, PhD Program in Software Eng., School of Computer Science Carnegie Mellon Univ., 2003; http://www-2.cs.cmu.edu/afs/cs.cmu.edu/project/isri/www/Design/phd.html.

[IEEE 1990] IEEE STD 610.12-1990, *IEEE Standard Glossary of Software Engineering Terminology*, IEEE Computer Soc., 1990.

[IEEE 2001a] Inst. for Electrical and Electronic Engineers. *IEEE Code of Ethics,* IEEE, May 2001; http://www.ieee.org/about/whatis/code.html.

[IEEE 2001b] ACM/IEEE Curriculum 2001 Task Force, *Computing Curricula 2001, Computer Science*, Dec. 2001; http://www.computer.org/education/cc2001/final/index.htm.

[IEEE 2003] Certified Software Development Professional, IEEE Computer Soc.; http://www.computer.org/certification/.

[JABEE 2003] Japan Accreditation Board for Eng., *Criteria for Accrediting Japanese Engineering Education Programs 2002-2003*; http://www.jabee.org/english/OpenHomePage/e_criteria&procedures.htm.

[Juristo 2003] N. Juristo, "Analysis of Software Engineering Degree Establishment in Europe," keynote address, 16th Conf. Software Eng. Education & Training, Mar. 2003; http://www.ls.fi.upm.es/cseet03/keynotes/Natalia_Juristo_CSEET03.pdf.

[Kelemen 1999] C.F. Kelemen, ed., *Computer Science Report to the CUPM Curriculum Foundations Workshop in Physics and Computer Science,* report from a workshop at Bowdoin College, Oct. 28-31, 1999.

[Kemper 1990] J. Kemper, *Engineers and Their Profession*, Oxford Univ. Press, 1990.

[King 1997] W.K. King and G. Engel, *Report on the Int'l Workshop on Computer Science and Eng. Accreditation*, IEEE Computer Soc., 1997

[Koffmanl 1984] E.P. Koffman, P.L. Miller, and C.E. Wardle, "Recommended Curriculum for CS1: 1984 Report of the ACM Curriculum Task Force for CS1," *Comm. ACM*, vol. 27, no. 10, Oct. 1984, pp. 998-1001.

[Koffman 1985] E.P. Koffman, D. Stemple, and C.E. Wardle, "Recommended Curriculum for CS2, 1984: A Report of the ACM Curriculum Task Force for CS2," *Comm. ACM*, vol. 28, no. 8, Aug. 1985, pp. 815-818.

[Lee 1998] E.A. Lee and D.G. Messerschmitt, "Engineering and Education for the Future," *Computer*, Jan. 1998, pp. 77-85.

[Lethbridge 2000] T. Lethbridge, "What Knowledge Is Important to a Software Engineer?" *Computer*, vol. 33, no. 6, May 2000, pp. 44-50.

[Lidtke 1999] D.K. Lidtke et al., *ISCC '99: An Information Systems-Centric Curriculum '99*, July 1999; http://www.iscc.unomaha.edu.

[Lutz 2001] M.J. Lutz, "Software Engineering on Internet Time," *Computer*, vol. 34, no. 5, May 2001, p. 36.

[Marciniak 1994] J. Marciniak, editor-in-chief, *Encyclopedia of Software Engineering*, John Wiley & Sons, 1994.

[Martin 1996] C.D. Martin et al., "Implementing a Tenth Strand in the CS Curriculum," *Comm. ACM*, vol. 39, no. 12, Dec. 1996, pp. 75-84.

[McConnell 1999] S. McConnell and L. Tripp, "Professional Software Engineering: Fact or Fiction?" *IEEE Software*, vol. 16, no. 6, Nov./Dec. 1999, pp. 13-17.

[McDermid 1991] J. McDermid, ed., *Software Engineer's Reference Book*, Butterworth-Heinemann Ltd., 1991.

[Meyer 2001 B. Meyer, "Software Engineering in the Academy," *Computer*, vol. 34, no. 5, May 2001, pp. 28-35.

[Mulder 1975] M.C. Mulder, "Model Curricula for Four-Year Computer Science and Engineering Programs: Bridging the Tar Pit," *Computer*, vol. 8, no. 12, Dec. 1975, pp. 28-33.

[Mulder 1984] M.C. Mulder and J. Dalphin, "Computer Science Program Requirements and Accreditation—an Interim Report of the ACM/IEEE Computer Society Joint Task Force," *Comm. ACM*, vol. 27, no. 4, Apr. 1984, pp. 330-335.

[Mulder 1998] F. Mulder and T. van Weert, "Informatics in Higher Education: Views on Informatics and Non-informatics Curricula," *Proc. IFIP/WG3.2 Working Conf. Informatics*

(Computer Science) as a Discipline and in Other Disciplines: What Is in Common?, Chapman and Hall, London, 1998.

[Myers 1997] C. Myers, T. Hall, and D. Pitt, eds., *Proc. 1st Westminster Conf.: Professional Awareness in Software Eng.* (PASE'96), London, Feb. 1996. (Published in edited form as *The Responsible Software Engineer*, Springer-Verlag, 1997).

[NACE 2003] Nat'l Assoc. of Colleges and Employers. *Job Outlook 2003*; http://www.naceweb.org/.

[Naur 1969] P. Naur and B. Randell, eds., *Software Engineering: Report on a Conference Sponsored by the NATO Science Committee*, Scientific Affairs Division, NATO, 1969.

[Naveda 1997] J.F. Naveda and M.J. Lutz, "The Road Less Travelled: A Baccalaureate Degree in Software Engineering," *Proc. 1997 Conf. Software Eng. Education & Training*, 1997.

[Neumann 1995] P.G. Neumann, *Computer Related Risks*, ACM Press, 1995.

[Nordheden 1999] K.J. Nordheden and M.H. Hoeflich, "Undergraduate Research & Intellectual Property Rights," *IEEE Trans. Education*, vol. 42, no. 4, 1999, p. 233.

[NSF 1996] Nat'l Science Foundation Advisory Committee, *Shaping the Future: New Expectations for Undergraduate Education in Science, Mathematics, Engineering, and Technology*, Nat'l Science Foundation, 1996.

[NTIA 1999] Nat'l Telecomm. and Information Administration, *Falling through the Net: Defining the Digital Divide*, Dept. of Commerce, Nov. 1999.

[Nunamaker 1982] J.F. Nunamaker Jr., J.D. Couger, and G.B. Davis, "Information Systems Curriculum Recommendations for the 80s: Undergraduate and Graduate Programs," *Comm. ACM*, vol. 25, no. 11, Nov. 1982, pp. 781-805.

[Oklobdzija 2002] V.G. Oklobdzija, ed., *The Computer Engineering Handbook*, CRC Press, 2002.

[OTA 1988] Office of Technology Assessment, *Educating Scientists and Engineers: Grade School to Grad School*, OTA-SET-377, US Government Printing Office, June 1988.

[QAA 2000] Quality Assurance Agency for Higher Education, *A Report on Benchmark Levels for Computing*, Southgate House, 2000.

[Parnas 1999] D.L. Parnas, "Software Engineering Programs Are Not Computer Science Programs," *IEEE Software*, Nov./Dec. 1999, pp. 19-30.

[Paulk 1995] M. Paulk et al., *The Capability Maturity Model: Guidelines for Improving the Software Process*, Addison-Wesley, 1995.

[PMI 2000] Project Management Institute, *Guide to the Project Management Body of Knowledge*, PMI, 2000.

[Ralston 2000] A. Ralston, E.D. Reilly, and D. Hemmendinger, eds., *Encyclopedia of Computer Science*, 4th ed., Nature Publishing Group, 2000.

[Ramamoorthy 1996] C.V. Ramamoorthy and W. Thai, "Advances in Software Engineering," *Comm. ACM*, vol. 29, no. 10, Oct. 1996, pp. 47-58.

[Richard 1999] W.D. Richard, D.E. Taylor, and D.M. Zar, "A Capstone Computer Engineering Design Course," *IEEE Trans. Education*, vol. 42, no. 4, Nov. 1999, pp. 288-294.

[Roberts 2001] E. Roberts and G. Engel, eds., *Computing Curricula 2001: Computer Science*, Report of the ACM and IEEE Computer Society Joint Task Force on Computing Curricula, final report, Dec. 2001.

[Roberts 1999] E. Roberts, "Conserving the Seed Corn: Reflections on the Academic Hiring Crisis," *SIGCSE Bulletin*, vol. 31, no. 4, Dec. 1999, pp. 4-9.

[Royce 1970] W.W. Royce, "Managing the Development of Large Software Systems: Concepts and Techniques," *Proc. WESCON*, Aug. 1970.

[SAC 1967] President's Science Advisory Commission, *Computers in Higher Education,* Washington DC: The White House, Feb. 1967.

[Saiedian 2002] H. Saiedian, D.J. Bagert, and N.R. Mead, "Software Eng. Programs: Dispelling the Myths and Misconceptions," *IEEE Software*, vol. 19 , no. 5, Sept./Oct. 2002, pp. 35-41.

[Shaw 1985] M. Shaw, *The Carnegie-Mellon Curriculum for Undergraduate Computer Science*, Springer-Verlag, 1985.

[Shaw 1990] M. Shaw, "Prospects for an Engineering Discipline of Software," *IEEE Software*, vol. 7, no. 6, Nov. 1990, pp. 15-24.

[Shaw 1991] M. Shaw and J.E. Tomayko. *Models for Undergraduate Courses in Software Engineering,* Software Eng. Inst., Carnegie Mellon Univ., Jan. 1991.

[Shaw 1992] M. Shaw, "We Can Teach Software Better," *Computing Research News*, vol. 4, no. 4, Sept. 1992, pp. 2-12.

[Shaw 2002] M. Shaw, "What Makes Good Research in Software Engineering?" *Int'l J. Software Tools for Technology Transfer*, vol. 4, DOI 10.1007/s10009-002-0083-4, June 2002.

[Shaw 2001] M. Shaw, "The Coming-of-Age of Software Architecture Research," *Proc 23rd Int'l Conf. Software Eng.,* IEEE Computer Soc., 2001, pp. 656-664a.

[SIGCHI 1992] Special Interest Group on Computer-Human Interaction, *ACM SIGCHI Curricula for Human-Computer Interaction*, ACM, 1992.

[Sobel 2002] A.E.K. Sobel and M. Clarkson, "Formal Methods Application: An Empirical Tale of Software Development," *IEEE Trans. Software Eng.*, vol. 28, no. 3, Mar. 2002.

[Sobel 2001] A.E.K. Sobel, "Emphasizing Mathematical Analysis in a Software Engineering Curriculum," *IEEE Trans. Education*, CD-ROM, vol. 44, no. 2, May 2001.

[Sobel 2000] A.E.K. Sobel, "Empirical Results of a Software Engineering Curriculum Incorporating Formal Methods," *Proc. SIGCSE*, Mar. 2000, pp. 157-161.

[Taipale, 1997] M. Taipale, ed., *Proc. Int'l Symp. Software Eng. in Universities (ISSEU'97)*, Rovaniemi, Finland, Mar. 1997.

[Thayer 1993] R.H. Thayer and A. McGettrick, eds., *Software Engineering—a European Perspective*, IEEE Computer Soc. Press, 1993.

[Thompson 2002] J.B. Thompson and H.M. Edwards, Preliminary Report on the CSEET 2002 Workshop "Developing the Software Engineering Volume of Computing Curriculum 2001", *Forum for Advancing Software Eng. Education (FASE)*, vol. 12, no. 3 (issue 146), Mar. 15, 2002.

[Thompson 2003] J.B. Thompson and H.M. Edwards, "Report on the 2nd International Summit on Software Engineering Education," *ACM SIGSOFT Software Eng. Notes*, vol. 28, issue 4 (July), 2003, pp. 21-26.

[Thompson 2004] J.B. Thompson, H.M. Edwards, and T.C. Lethbridge, *Post-Summit Proc. Int'l Summit on Software Eng. Education (SSEE)*, Univ. of Sunderland Press, Sunderland, UK, 2004.

[Tomayko 1999] J.E. Tomayko, "Forging a Discipline: An Outline History of Software Engineering Education," *Annals of Software Eng.*, vol. 6, no. 1-4, Apr. 1999, pp. 3-18.

[Tremblay 2000] G. Tremblay, "Formal Methods: Mathematics, Computer Science, or Software Engineering?" *IEEE Trans. Education*, vol. 43, no. 4, Nov. 2000, pp. 377-382.

[Tucker 1991] A.B. Tucker et al., *Computing Curricula '91*, Assoc. for Computing Machinery and the IEEE Computer Soc., 1991.

[Umphress 2002] D.A. Umphress, T.D. Hendrix, and J.H. Cross, "Software Process in the Classroom: The Capstone Project Experience," *IEEE Software*, vol. 19 , no. 5, Sept./Oct. 2002, pp. 78-85.

[Walker 1996] H.M. Walker and G.M. Schneider, "A Revised Model Curriculum for a Liberal Arts Degree in Computer Science," *Comm. ACM*, vol. 39, no. 12, Dec. 1996, pp. 85-95.

[Zadeh 1968] L.A. Zade, "Computer Science as a Discipline," *J. Eng. Education*, vol. 58, no. 8, Apr. 1968, pp. 913-916.

Appendix A: Detailed Descriptions of Proposed Courses

In this appendix, we provide details of the courses referred to in chapter 6. Some of the courses are taken from the CCCS volume, whereas others are new courses being introduced in this software engineering volume. For the new courses, the following is provided: a full course description, a list of prerequisites, learning objectives, and a listing of the anticipated coverage of SEEK (chapter 4) provided by the course. In some cases, teaching modules, suggested labs and exercises, and other pedagogical guidance is provided. For CCCS courses, we just list the SEEK coverage.

In most cases, coverage of SEEK is considerably less than the 40 lecture-equivalent-hours that is used as a benchmark for a "complete" course. This leaves space for institutions and instructors to tailor the courses, covering extra material or covering the given material in more depth.

CCCS introductory courses

Because these courses are taken directly from the CCCS volume, the reader should consult that volume for more details [IEEE 2001b] . Note that other CCCS courses could be substituted for these.

CS101₁ Programming Fundamentals

This course is taken directly from the Computer Science volume (CCCS)

Course description:
Introduces the fundamental concepts of procedural programming. Topics include data types, control structures, functions, arrays, files, and the mechanics of running, testing, and debugging. The course also offers an introduction to the historical and social context of computing and an overview of computer science as a discipline.
Prerequisites: No programming or computer science experience is required. Students should have sufficient facility with high-school mathematics to solve simple linear equations and to appreciate the use of mathematical notation and formalism.
Syllabus:

- Computing applications: Word processing, spreadsheets, editors, files and directories

- Fundamental programming constructs: Syntax and semantics of a higher-level language; variables, types, expressions, and assignment; simple I/O; conditional and iterative control structures; functions and parameter passing; structured decomposition

- Algorithms and problem-solving: Problem-solving strategies, the role of algorithms in the problem-solving process, implementation strategies for algorithms, debugging strategies, the concept and properties of algorithms

- Fundamental data structures: Primitive types, arrays, records, strings and string processing

- Machine level representation of data: Bits, bytes, and words; numeric data representation and number bases; representation of character data

- Overview of operating systems: The role and purpose of operating systems, simple file management

- Introduction to net-centric computing: Background and history of networking and the Internet; demonstration and use of networking software including e-mail, telnet, and FTP

- Human–computer interaction: Introduction to design issues

- Software development methodology: Fundamental design concepts and principles, structured design, testing and debugging strategies, test-case design, programming environments, testing and debugging tools

- Social context of computing: History of computing and computers; evolution of ideas and machines; social impact of computers and the Internet; professionalism, codes of ethics, and responsible conduct; copyrights, intellectual property, and software piracy.

Total hours of SEEK coverage: 39
CMP.cf (30 core hours of 140): Computer science foundations
  CMP.cf.1 (13 core hours of 39): Programming fundamentals
  CMP.cf.2 (3 core hours of 31): Algorithms, data structures/representation
  CMP.cf.3 (2 core hours of 5): Problem-solving techniques
  CMP.cf.6 (1 core hour of 1): Basic concept of a system
  CMP.cf.7 (1 core hour of 1): Basic user human factors
  CMP.cf.8 (1 core hour of 1): Basic developer human factors
  CMP.cf.9 (7 core hours of 12): Programming language basics
  CMP.cf.10 (1 core hour of 10): Operating system basics key concepts from CCCS
  CMP.cf.12 (1 core hour of 5): Network communication basics
CMP.tl (1 core hour of 4): Construction tools
PRF.pr (4 core hours of 20): Professionalism
  PRF.pr.2: Codes of ethics and professional conduct
  PRF.pr.3: Social, legal, historical, and professional issues and concerns
  PRF.pr.6: The economic impact of software
MAA.rfd (1 core hour of 3): Requirements fundamentals
DES.con (1 core hour of 3): Software design concepts
  DES.con.1: Definition of design
VAV.rev (1 core hour of 6): Reviews
  VAV.rev.1: Desk checking
VAV.tst (1 core hour of 21): Testing
  VAV.tst.1: Unit testing

CS102₁ The Object-Oriented Paradigm

This course is taken directly from the Computer Science volume (CCCS)

Course description:
Introduces the concept of object-oriented programming to students with a background in the procedural paradigm. The course begins with a review of control structures and data types with emphasis on structured data types and array processing. It then moves on to introduce the object-oriented programming paradigm, focusing on the definition and use of classes along with the fundamentals of object-oriented design. Other topics include an overview of programming language principles, simple analysis of algorithms, basic searching and sorting techniques, and an introduction to software engineering issues.

Prerequisites: CS101ı

Syllabus:

- Review of control structures, functions, and primitive data types

- Object-oriented programming: Object-oriented design; encapsulation and information-hiding; separation of behavior and implementation; classes, subclasses, and inheritance; polymorphism; class hierarchies

- Fundamental computing algorithms: simple searching and sorting algorithms (linear and binary search, selection and insertion sort)

- Fundamentals of event-driven programming

- Introduction to computer graphics: Using a simple graphics API

- Overview of programming languages: History of programming languages, brief survey of programming paradigms

- Virtual machines: The concept of a virtual machine, hierarchy of virtual machines, intermediate languages

- Introduction to language translation: Comparison of interpreters and compilers, language translation phases, machine-dependent and machine-independent aspects of translation

- Introduction to database systems: History and motivation for database systems, use of a database query language

- Software evolution: Software maintenance, characteristics of maintainable software, reengineering, legacy systems, software reuse

Total hours of SEEK coverage: 36
CMP.cf (30 core hours of 140): Computer science foundations
  CMP.cf.1 (13 core hours of 39): Programming fundamentals
  CMP.cf.2 (3 core hours of 31): Algorithms, data structures/representation
  CMP.cf.3 (3 core hours of 5): Problem-solving techniques
  CMP.cf.4 (3 core hours of 5): Abstraction—use and support for
  CMP.cf.5 (2 core hours of 20): Computer organization
  CMP.cf.9 (5 core hours of 12): Programming language basics
  CMP.cf.11 (1 core hour of 10): Database basics
CMP.ct (1 core hour of 20): Construction technologies
  DES.con.4: Design principles
DES.hci (3 core hours of 12): Human–computer interface design
  DES.hci.1: General HCI design principles
VAV.fnd (1 core hour of 5): V&V terminology and foundations
  VAV.fnd.1: Objectives and constraints of V&V
EVO.pro (1 core hour of 6): Evolution processes
  EVO.pro.1: Basic concepts of evolution and maintenance

CS103 Data Structures and Algorithms

This course is taken directly from the Computer Science volume (CCCS)

Course description:
Builds on the foundation provided by the CS101I-102I sequence to introduce the fundamental concepts of data structures and the algorithms that proceed from them. Topics include recursion, the underlying philosophy of object-oriented programming, fundamental data structures (including stacks, queues, linked lists, hash tables, trees, and graphs), the basics of algorithmic analysis, and an introduction to the principles of language translation.

Prerequisites: CS102I; discrete mathematics at the level of CS105 is also desirable.

Syllabus:

- Review of elementary programming concepts

- Fundamental data structures: Stacks, queues, linked lists, hash tables, trees, graphs

- Object-oriented programming: Object-oriented design, encapsulation and information hiding, classes, separation of behavior and implementation, class hierarchies, inheritance, polymorphism

- Fundamental computing algorithms: O(N log N) sorting algorithms; hash tables, including collision-avoidance strategies; binary search trees; representations of graphs; depth- and breadth-first traversals

- Recursion: The concept of recursion, recursive mathematical functions, simple recursive procedures, divide-and-conquer strategies, recursive backtracking, implementation of recursion

- Basic algorithmic analysis: Asymptotic analysis of upper and average complexity bounds; identifying differences between best-, average-, and worst-case behaviors; big "O," little "o," omega, and theta notation; standard complexity classes; empirical measurements of performance; time and space trade-offs in algorithms; using recurrence relations to analyze recursive algorithms

- Algorithmic strategies: Brute-force algorithms, greedy algorithms, divide-and-conquer, backtracking, branch-and-bound, heuristics, pattern matching and string/text algorithms, numerical approximation algorithms

- Overview of programming languages: Programming paradigms

- Software engineering: Software validation; testing fundamentals, including test plan creation and test case generation; object-oriented testing

Total hours of SEEK coverage: 31
CMP.cf (30 core hours of 140): Computer science foundations
   CMP.cf.1 (13 core hours of 39): Programming fundamentals
   CMP.cf.2 (15 core hours of 31): Algorithms, data structures/representation
   CMP.cf.4 (2 core hours of 5): Abstraction—use and support for
   CMP.cf.9: Programming language basics
VAV.tst (1 core hour of 21): Testing
   VAV.tst.2: Exception handling

This is a sample of CCCS courses that can be used to teach required material in SEEK. Other combinations of CCCS courses could be used, or new courses could be created to cover the same material. If this particular sequence of three courses is used, the students will be taught much material beyond the essentials specified in SEEK. We believe many software engineering programs will want to provide as much computer science as this, or even more.

CS220 Computer Architecture

This course is taken directly from the CCCS volume.

Course description:
Introduces students to the organization and architecture of computer systems, beginning with the standard von Neumann model and then moving forward to more recent architectural concepts.
Prerequisites: Introduction to computer science (any implementation of CS103 or CS112), discrete structures (CS106 or CS115)
Syllabus:

- Digital logic: Fundamental building blocks (logic gates, flip-flops, counters, registers, PLA); logic expressions, minimization, sum of product forms; register transfer notation; physical considerations (gate delays, fan-in, fan-out)

- Data representation: Bits, bytes, and words; numeric data representation and number bases; fixed- and floating-point systems; signed and twos-complement representations; representation of nonnumeric data (character codes, graphical data); representation of records and arrays

- Assembly-level organization: Basic organization of the von Neumann machine; control unit; instruction fetch, decode, and execution; instruction sets and types (data manipulation, control, I/O); assembly/machine language programming; instruction formats; addressing modes; subroutine call and return mechanisms; I/O and interrupts

- Memory systems: Storage systems and their technology; coding, data compression, and data integrity; memory hierarchy; main memory organization and operations; latency, cycle time, bandwidth, and interleaving; cache memories (address mapping, block size, replacement and store policy); virtual memory (page table, TLB); fault handling and reliability

- Interfacing and communication: I/O fundamentals: handshaking, buffering, programmed I/O, interrupt-driven I/O; interrupt structures: vectored and prioritized, interrupt acknowledgment; external storage, physical organization, and drives; buses: bus protocols, arbitration, direct-memory access (DMA); introduction to networks; multimedia support; raid architectures

- Functional organization: Implementation of simple data paths; control unit: hardwired realization vs. microprogrammed realization; instruction pipelining; introduction to instruction-level parallelism (ILP)

- Multiprocessor and alternative architectures: Introduction to SIMD, MIMD, VLIW, EPIC; systolic architecture; interconnection networks; shared memory systems; cache coherence; memory models and memory consistency

- Performance enhancements: RISC architecture, branch prediction, prefetching, scalability

- Contemporary architectures: Handheld devices, embedded systems, trends in processor architecture

Total hours of SEEK coverage: 15
CMP.cf (15 core hours of 140): Computer science foundations
CMP.cf.5 (15 core hours of 20): Computer organization

CS226 Operating Systems and Networking

This course is taken directly from the CCCS volume.

Course description:
Introduces the fundamentals of operating systems together with the basics of networking and communications.
Prerequisites: Introduction to computer science (any implementation of CS103 or CS112), discrete structures (CS106 or CS115)
Syllabus:

- Introduction to event-driven programming

- Using APIs: API programming, class browsers and related tools, programming by example, debugging in the API environment

- Overview of operating systems: Role and purpose of the operating system, history of operating system development, functionality of a typical operating system

- Operating system principles: Structuring methods; abstractions, processes, and resources; concepts of application program interfaces; device organization; interrupts; concepts of user/system state and protection

- Introduction to concurrency: Synchronization principles, the "mutual exclusion" problem and some solutions, deadlock avoidance

- Introduction to concurrency: States and state diagrams, structures, dispatching and context switching, the role of interrupts, concurrent execution, the "mutual exclusion" problem and some solutions, deadlock, models and mechanisms, producer-consumer problems and synchronization

- Scheduling and dispatch: Preemptive and nonpreemptive scheduling, schedulers and policies, processes and threads, deadlines and real-time issues

- Memory management: Review of physical memory and memory management hardware; overlays, swapping, and partitions; paging and segmentation; placement and replacement policies; working sets and thrashing; caching

- Introduction to distributed algorithms: Consensus and election, fault tolerance

- Introduction to net-centric computing: Background and history of networking and the Internet, network architectures, the range of specializations within net-centric computing

- Introduction to networking and communications: Network architectures, issues associated with distributed computing, simple network protocols, APIs for network operations

- Introduction to the World-Wide Web: Web technologies, characteristics of Web servers, nature of the client-server relationship, Web protocols, support tools for Web site creation and Web management

- Network security: Fundamentals of cryptography, secret-key algorithms, public-key algorithms, authentication protocols, digital signatures, examples

Total hours of SEEK coverage: 16
CMP.cf (16 core hours of 140): Computer science foundations
CMP.cf.2 (3 core hours of 31): Algorithms, data structures/representation
CMP.cf.10 (9 core hours of 10): Operating system basics key concepts from CCCS
CMP.cf.12 (4 core hours of 5): Network communication basics

CS270T Databases

This course is taken directly from the CCCS volume.

Course description:
Introduces the concepts and techniques of database systems.
Prerequisites: Introduction to computer science (any implementation of CS103 or CS112), discrete structures (CS106 or CS115)
Syllabus:

- Information models and systems: History and motivation for information systems; information storage and retrieval; information management applications; information capture and representation; analysis and indexing; search, retrieval, linking, and navigation; information privacy, integrity, security, and preservation; scalability, efficiency, and effectiveness

- Database systems: History and motivation for database systems, components of database systems, DBMS functions, database architecture and data independence

- Data modeling: Data modeling, conceptual models, object-oriented model, relational data model

- Relational databases: Mapping conceptual schema to a relational schema, entity and referential integrity, relational algebra and relational calculus

- Database query languages: Overview of database languages, SQL, query optimization, fourth-generation environments, embedding nonprocedural queries in a procedural language, introduction to Object Query Language

- Relational database design: Database design, functional dependency, normal forms, multivalued dependency, join dependency, representation theory

- Transaction processing: Transactions, failure and recovery, concurrency control

- Distributed databases: Distributed data storage, distributed query processing, distributed transaction model, concurrency control, homogeneous and heterogeneous solutions, client-server

- Physical database design: Storage and file structure, indexed files, hashed files, signature files, b-trees, files with dense index, files with variable length records, database efficiency and tuning

Total hours of SEEK coverage: 13
CMP.cf (11 core hours of 140): Computer science foundations
  CMP.cf.2 (2 core hours of 31): Algorithms, data structures/representation
  CMP.cf.11 (9 core hours of 10): Database basics
MAA.md (2 core hours of 19): Modeling

```
┌─────────────────────────────────────────────┐
│         Mathematics fundamentals courses      │
└─────────────────────────────────────────────┘
```

CS105 Discrete Structures I

This course is taken directly from the CCCS volume.

Course description:
Introduces the foundations of discrete mathematics as they apply to computer science, focusing on providing a solid theoretical foundation for further work. Topics include functions, relations, sets, simple proof techniques, Boolean algebra, propositional logic, digital logic, elementary number theory, and the fundamentals of counting.
Prerequisites: Mathematical preparation sufficient to take calculus at the college level.
Syllabus:

- Introduction to logic and proofs: Direct proofs, proof by contradiction, mathematical induction

- Fundamental structures: Functions (surjections, injections, inverses, composition), relations (reflexivity, symmetry, transitivity, equivalence relations), sets (Venn diagrams, complements, Cartesian products, power sets), pigeonhole principle, cardinality and countability

- Boolean algebra: Boolean values, standard operations on Boolean values, de Morgan's laws

- Propositional logic: Logical connectives, truth tables, normal forms (conjunctive and disjunctive), validity

- Digital logic: Logic gates, flip-flops, counters; circuit minimization

- Elementary number theory: Factorability, properties of primes, greatest common divisors and least common multiples, Euclid's algorithm, modular arithmetic, the Chinese Remainder Theorem

- Basics of counting: Counting arguments, pigeonhole principle, permutations and combinations, binomial coefficients

Total hours of SEEK coverage: 24

CMP.cf (3 core hours of 140): Computer science foundations
  CMP.cf.5 (3 core hours of 20): Computer organization
FND.mf (21 core hours of 56): Mathematical foundations
  FND.mf.1 (6 core hours of 6): Functions, relations, and sets
  FND.mf.2 (5 core hours of 9): Basic logic
  FND.mf.3 (4 core hours of 9): Proof techniques
  FND.mf.4 (6 core hours of 6): Basic counting
  FND.mf.10: Number theory

CS106 Discrete Structures II

This course is taken directly from the CCCS volume.

Course description:
Continues the discussion of discrete mathematics introduced in CS105. Topics in the second course include predicate logic, recurrence relations, graphs, trees, matrices, computational complexity, elementary computability, and discrete probability.
Prerequisites: CS105
Syllabus:

- Review of previous course

- Predicate logic: Universal and existential quantification, modus ponens and modus tollens, limitations of predicate logic

- Recurrence relations: Basic formulae, elementary solution techniques

- Graphs and trees: Fundamental definitions, simple algorithms, traversal strategies, proof techniques, spanning trees, applications

- Matrices: Basic properties, applications

- Computational complexity: Order analysis, standard complexity classes

- Elementary computability: Countability and uncountability, diagonalization proof to show uncountability of the reals, definition of the P and NP classes, simple demonstration of the halting problem

- Discrete probability: Finite probability spaces; conditional probability, independence, Bayes' rule; random events; random integer variables; mathematical expectation

Total hours of SEEK coverage: 27
CMP.cf (5 core hours of 140): Computer science foundations
  CMP.cf.2 (5 core hours of 31): Algorithms, data structures/representation
FND.mf (19 core hours of 56): Mathematical foundations
  FND.mf.2 (4 core hours of 9): Basic logic
  FND.mf.3 (5 core hours of 9): Proof techniques
  FND.mf.4 (0 core hours of 6): Basic counting
  FND.mf.5 (4 core hours of 5): Graphs and trees
  FND.mf.6 (6 core hours of 9): Discrete probability
MAA.md (3 core hours of 19): Modeling

MA271 Statistics and Empirical Methods for Computing

This is a new course introduced as part of this Software Engineering volume, even though the topics covered are not in the domain of software engineering per se. The need for this course is motivated by a desire to teach basic probability and statistics in an applied manner that will be seen as relevant to software engineering students. It might be possible to substitute a more generic statistics course, but the experience of many educators is that students easily forget their statistics background because they do not see how it is relevant to their chosen career. It is hoped that this course will rectify that to some extent.

Course description:
Principles of discrete probability with applications to computing. Basics of descriptive statistics. Distributions, including normal (Gaussian), binomial, and Poisson. Least squared concept, correlation and regression. Statistical tests most useful to software engineering: t-test, ANOVA, and chi-squared. Design of experiments and testing of hypotheses. Statistical analysis of data from a variety of sources. Applications of statistics to performance analysis, reliability engineering, usability engineering, cost estimation, as well as process control evaluation.

Learning objectives:
Upon completion of this course, students will have the ability to:

- Make design and management decisions based on a good understanding of probability and statistics

- Design and conduct experiments to evaluate hypotheses about software quality and process

- Analyze data from a variety of sources

- Appreciate the importance of empirical methods in software engineering

Sample labs and assignments:

- Building spreadsheets using data gathered from experiments of various kinds, and using native statistical functions in spreadsheets to assist in hypothesis testing

- Use of statistics applications such as SAS or SPSS

Additional teaching considerations:

- Some educators like to show the derivation of statistical techniques from first principles, and spend much time in a statistics course discussing and proving theorems. We suggest that material taught in this way tends to be readily forgotten by all but the most mathematically inclined computing students, and is therefore often a waste of time. We suggest instead, that statistics techniques be taught as "cookbook" methods, although with enough of their rationale explained so students can subsequently expand their knowledge. Using this approach, students can in a later (optional) course be taught more of the mathematical underpinnings of statistics and/or a wider variety of data analysis techniques.

- The use of spreadsheets, in addition to statistical applications is suggested, since all software companies have spreadsheet software, but not all have, or are willing to obtain, the more powerful, complex, and expensive statistics applications. Students will be more likely to believe they can apply statistics later if they know how to do it using spreadsheets.

- This course could be linked to other SE courses being taught in parallel, for example SE212, SE321, or SE323. Whether or not those courses are taught in parallel, they should also provide exercises to reinforce the material learned in this course.

Total hours of SEEK coverage: 18
FND.mf (3 core hours of 56): Mathematical foundations
   FND.mf.6 (3 core hours of 9): Discrete probability
FND.ef (15 core hours of 23): Engineering foundations for software
   FND.ef.1: Empirical methods and experimental techniques
   FND.ef.2: Statistical analysis

Nontechnical (NT) compulsory courses

In the following series of courses, total SEEK coverage in each course is far less than 40 hours, so institutions have considerable freedom to tailor the courses to more closely fit their needs.

NT272 Engineering Economics

Courses like this are widely taught in engineering faculties, particularly in North America. The course presented below can be used in an engineering program for any type of engineering. It could be tailored more specifically to the needs of software engineering.

Course description:
The scope of engineering economics; mesoeconomics; supply, demand, and production; cost-benefit analysis and break-even analysis; return on investment; analysis of options; time value of money; management of money: economic analysis, accounting for risk.

Learning objectives:
Upon completion of this course, students will have the ability to:

- Analyze supply and demand for products

- Perform simple break-even analyses

- Perform simple cost-benefit analyses

- Analyze the economic effect of alternative investment decisions, marketing decisions, and design decisions, considering the time value of money and potential risk

Total hours of SEEK coverage: 13
FND.ef (2 core hours of 23): Engineering foundations for software
   FND.ef.5: Engineering design
FND.ec (10 core hours of 10): Engineering economics for software
MGT.pp (1 core hour of 6): Project planning

NT181 Group Dynamics and Communication

Course description:

Essentials of oral, written, and graphical communication for software engineers. Principles of technical writing; types of documents and strategies for gathering information and writing documents, including presentations. Appropriate use of tables, graphics, and references. How to be convincing and how to express rationale for one's decisions or conclusions. Basics of how to work effectively with others; notion of what motivates people; concepts of group dynamics. Principles of effective oral communication, both at the interpersonal level and when making presentations to groups. Strategies for listening, persuasion, and negotiation.

Learning objectives:
Upon completion of this course, students will have the ability to:

- Write clear, concise, and accurate technical documents following well-defined standards for format and for including appropriate tables, figures, and references

- Review written technical documentation to detect problems of various kinds

- Develop and deliver a good quality formal presentation

- Negotiate basic agreements with peers

- Participate in interactions with others in which they are able to get their point across and are also able to listen to and appreciate the points of others, even when they disagree, and are able to convey to others that they have listened

Additional teaching considerations:

- Some students will have poor writing skills, so one objective of this course should be to help students improve those skills. However, it is suggested that remedial help in grammar, sentence structure, and so on, should not be part of the main course, because it will waste the time of those students who do not need it. Remedial writing help should, therefore, be available separately for those who need it. The writing of all students should be very critically judged; it should not be possible to pass this course unless the student learns to write well.

- Instructors should have students write several documents of moderate size, emphasizing clarity, usefulness, and writing quality. It is suggested that complex document formats be avoided.

- Students could be asked to write requirements, to describe how something works, or to describe how to do something. These topics will best prepare students for the types of writing they will need to do as a software engineer. The topics assigned should be interesting to students, so that they feel more motivated: For example, they could be asked to describe a game.

Total hours of SEEK coverage: 11
PRF.psy (3 core hours of 5): Group dynamics/psychology
PRF.com (8 core hours of 10): Communications skills
  MAA.rsd.1: Requirements documentation basics

NT291 Professional Software Engineering Practice

Course description:

History of computing and software engineering. Principles of professional software engineering practice and ethics. Societal and environmental obligations of the software engineer. Role of professional organizations. Intellectual property and other laws relevant to software engineering practice.

Learning objectives:
Upon completion of this course, students will have the ability to:

- Make ethical decisions when faced with ethical dilemmas, with reference to general principles of ethics as well as codes of ethics for engineering, computing, and software engineering

- Apply concern for safety, security, and human rights to engineering and management decision-making

- Understand basics of the history of engineering, computing, and software engineering

- Describe and apply the laws that affect software engineers, including laws regarding copyright, patents, and other intellectual property

- Describe the effect of software engineering decisions on society, the economy, the environment, their customers, their management, their peers, and themselves

- Describe the importance of the various different professional societies relevant to software engineering in the state, province or country, as well as internationally

- Understand the role of standards and standards-making bodies in engineering and software engineering

- Understand the need for continual professional development as an engineer and a software engineer

Additional teaching considerations:

- It is suggested that this course be taught in part using presentations by guest speakers. For example, there could be talks by an expert on ethics, a representative of a professional society, and an intellectual property expert.

- Students should be asked to read and discuss articles relevant to the course from the popular, trade, and academic presses.

- Students should be asked to debate various ethical issues.

- Care should be taken to present both sides of certain issues. In particular, we feel that the case both for and against the licensing of software engineers should be presented, because respected leaders of the profession still have diametrically opposite views on this. Another issue where it is important to present both sides is patenting of software. We believe it is entirely acceptable for the instructor to present his or her "political" opinions on these issues as long as students can also learn how the "other side" thinks and are not penalized for opposing the instructor's views.

Total hours of SEEK coverage: 14
PRF.pr (13 core hours of 20): Professionalism

PRF.pr.1: Accreditation, certification, and licensing
PRF.pr.2: Codes of ethics and professional conduct
PRF.pr.3: Social, legal, historical, and professional issues and concerns
PRF.pr.4: The nature and role of professional societies
PRF.pr.5: The nature and role of software engineering standards
PRF.pr.6: The economic impact of software
QUA.cc (1 core hour of 2): Software quality concepts and culture
QUA.cc.2: Society's concern for quality
QUA.cc.3: The costs and impacts of bad quality

SE+CS introductory courses—first year start

SE101 Introduction to Software Engineering and Computing

This course is a first course in computing, taught with a software engineering emphasis. It is designed to be taught with SE102 as replacements for any of the CS101 and CS102 courses from the CCCS volume. The CS courses do teach software engineering basics; however, the idea is that this course would start with the SE material, and teach all the material as a means to the end of solving software engineering problems for customers.

Course Description:
Overview of software engineering: Systems, customers, users, and their requirements. General principles of computing: Problem solving, abstraction, division of the system into manageable components, reuse, simple interfaces. Programming concepts: Control constructs; expressions; use of APIs; simple data including arrays and strings; classes and inheritance. Design concepts: Evaluation of alternatives. Basics of testing.
Prerequisites: High school education with good grades and a sense of rigor and attention to detail developed through science and mathematics courses.

Learning objectives:
Upon completion of this course, students will have the ability to:

- Develop simple statements of requirements

- Appreciate the advantage of alternative sets of requirements and designs for very simple programs

- Write small programs in some language

- Systematically test and debug small programs

Additional teaching considerations: Because this is a first course in computing, the challenge will be to motivate students about software engineering before they know very much about programming. One way to do this is to study simple programs from the outside (as black boxes), looking at the features they provide and discussing how they could be improved. This needs to be done, though, with sufficient academic rigor.

The course could be approached in two parallel streams (that is, two mini-courses that are synchronized). One stream looks at higher-level software engineering issues, while another teaches programming.

Total hours of SEEK coverage: 35
CMP.cf (19 core hours of 140): Computer science foundations
  CMP.cf.1 (9 core hours of 39): Programming fundamentals
  CMP.cf.3 (2 core hours of 5): Problem-solving techniques
  CMP.cf.4 (1 core hour of 5): Abstraction—use and support for
  CMP.cf.5 (2 core hours of 20): Computer organization
  CMP.cf.6 (1 core hour of 1): Basic concept of a system
  CMP.cf.7 (1 core hour of 1): Basic user-human factors
  CMP.cf.8 (1 core hour of 1) : Basic developer-human factors
  CMP.cf.9 (2 core hours of 12): Programming language basics
CMP.ct (2 core hours of 20): Construction technologies
CMP.tl (1 core hour of 4): Construction tools
FND.ef (2 core hours of 23): Engineering foundations for software
  FND.ef.3: Measuring individual's performance
  FND.ef.4: Systems development
  FND.ef.5: Engineering design
PRF.pr (2 core hours of 20): Professionalism
MAA.tm (1 core hour of 12): Types of models
MAA.rfd (2 core hours of 3): Requirements fundamentals
MAA.er (1 core hour of 4): Eliciting requirements
MAA.rsd (1 core hour of 6): Requirements specification & documentation
DES.con (1 core hour of 3): Software design concepts
DES.str (1 core hour of 6): Software design strategies
DES.dd (1 core hour of 12): Detailed design
VAV.tst (1 core hour of 21): Testing

SE102 Software Engineering and Computing II

This course is the successor to SE101 for students following a software-oriented introductory computing sequence

Course Description:
Requirements, design, implementation, reviewing, and testing of simple software that interacts with the operating system, databases, and network, and that involves graphical user interfaces. Use of simple data structures, such as stacks and queues. Effective use of the facilities of a programming language. Design and analysis of simple algorithms, including those using recursion. Use of simple design patterns such as delegation. Drawing simple UML class, package, and component diagrams. Dealing with change: Evolution principles; handling requirements changes; problem reporting and tracking.

Prerequisite: SE101

Learning objectives:
Upon completion of this course, students will have the ability to:

- Develop clear, concise, and sufficiently formal requirements for extensions to an existing system, based on the true needs of users and other stakeholders

- Design software, so that it can be changed easily

- Design simple algorithms with recursion

- Analyze basic algorithms to determine their efficiency

- Draw simple diagrams representing software designs

- Write medium-sized programs, in teams

- Develop simple graphical user interfaces

- Conduct inspections of medium-sized programs

Additional teaching considerations:
As with SE101, students need to be reminded regularly of the principles of software engineering.

Total hours of SEEK coverage: 36
CMP.cf (23 core hours of 140): Computer science foundations
  CMP.cf.1 (12 core hours of 39): Programming fundamentals
  CMP.cf.3 (3 core hours of 5): Problem-solving techniques
  CMP.cf.4 (1 core hour of 5): Abstraction–use and support for
  CMP.cf.9 (4 core hours of 12): Programming language basics
  CMP.cf.10 (1 core hour of 10): Operating system basics key concepts from CCCS
  CMP.cf.11 (1 core hour of 10): Database basics
  CMP.cf.12 (1 core hour of 5): Network communication basics
PRF.pr (1 core hour of 20): Professionalism
MAA.md (1 core hour of 19): Modeling
MAA.rv (1 core hour of 3): Requirements validation
DES.str (1 core hour of 6): Software design strategies
DES.dd (1 core hour of 12): Detailed design
DES.nst (1 core hours of 3): Design notations and support tools
VAV.fnd (1 core hour of 5): V&V terminology and foundations
VAV.rev (1 core hour of 6): Reviews
VAV.tst (2 core hours of 21): Testing
VAV.par (1 core hour of 4): Problem analysis and reporting
EVO.pro (1 core hour of 6): Evolution processes

SE200 Software Engineering and Computing III

This is a third course for students who have followed the sequence SE101 and SE102.

Course Description:
Software process, planning and tracking one's work. Analysis, architecture, and design of simple client-server systems using UML, with an emphasis on class and state diagrams. Evaluating designs. Implementing designs using appropriate data structures, frameworks, and APIs.
Prerequisite: SE102

Learning objectives:
Upon completion of this course, students will have the ability to:

- Plan the development of a simple system

- Measure and track their progress while developing software

- Create good UML class and state diagrams

- Implement systems of significant complexity

Additional teaching considerations:
This course is a good place to start to expose students to moderately sized existing systems. They can therefore learn and practice the essential skills of reading and understanding code written by others.

In contrast with SE201, this course should balance SE learning with continued learning of programming and basic computer science.

It is suggested that a core subset of UML be taught, rather than trying to cover all features.

Total hours of SEEK coverage: 38
CMP.cf (18 core hours of 140): Computer science foundations
   CMP.cf.1 (5 core hours of 39): Programming fundamentals
   CMP.cf.2 (6 core hours of 31): Algorithms, data structures/representation
   CMP.cf.4 (1 core hour of 5): Abstraction—use and support for
   CMP.cf.9 (6 core hours of 12): Programming language basics
CMP.ct (3 core hours of 20): Construction technologies
FND.ef (1 core hour of 23): Engineering foundations for software
PRF.pr (2 core hours of 20): Professionalism
MAA.md (1 core hour of 19): Modeling
DES.con (2 core hours of 3): Software design concepts
DES.str (1 core hour of 6): Software design strategies
DES.ar (2 core hours of 9): Architectural design
DES.hci (4 core hours of 12): Human–computer interface design
DES.ev (1 core hour of 3): Design evaluation
VAV.fnd (1 core hour of 5): V&V terminology and foundations

VAV.rev (1 core hour of 6): Reviews
PRO.imp (1 core hour of 10): Process implementation
MGT.con (1 core hour of 2): Management concepts

SE201 Introduction to Software Engineering

This is a first course in software engineering for students who have taken CS101 and CS102.

Course description:
Principles of software engineering: Requirements, design, and testing. Review of principles of object orientation. Object-oriented analysis using UML. Frameworks and APIs. Introduction to the client-server architecture. Analysis, design, and programming of simple servers and clients. Introduction to user interface technology.
Prerequisite: CS102

Learning objectives
Upon completion of this course, students will have the ability to:

- Develop clear, concise, and sufficiently formal requirements for extensions to an existing system, based on the true needs of users and other stakeholders

- Apply design principles and patterns while designing and implementing simple distributed systems based on reusable technology

- Create UML class diagrams that model aspects of the domain and the software architecture

- Create UML sequence diagrams and state machines that correctly model system behavior

- Implement a simple graphical user interfaces for a system

- Apply simple measurement techniques to software

- Demonstrate an appreciation for the breadth of software engineering

Suggested sequence of teaching modules:
1. Software engineering and its place as an engineering discipline
2. Review of the principles of object orientation
3. Reusable technologies as a basis for software engineering: Frameworks and APIs. Introduction to client-server computing
4. Requirements analysis
5. UML class diagrams and object-oriented analysis; introduction to formal modeling using OCL
6. Examples of building class diagrams to model various domains
7. Design patterns (abstraction-occurrence, composite, player-role, singleton, observer, delegation, façade, adapter, observer, and so on)
8. Use cases and user-centered design
9. Representing software behavior: Sequence diagrams, state machines, activity diagrams
10. General software design principles: Decomposition, decoupling, cohesion, reuse, reusability, portability, testability, flexibility, and so on
11. Software architecture: Distributed architectures, pipe-and-filter, model-view-controller, and so on
12. Introduction to testing and project management

Sample labs and assignments:

- Evaluating the performance of various simple software designs

- Adding features to an existing system

- Testing a system to verify conformance to test cases

- Building a GUI for an application

- Numerous exercises building models in UML, particularly class diagrams and state machines

- Developing a simple set of requirements (to be done as a team) for some innovative client-server application of very small size

- Implementing the above, using reusable technology to the greatest extent possible

Additional teaching considerations:
This course is a good place to start to expose students to moderately sized existing systems. With such systems, they can learn and practice the essential skills of reading and understanding code written by others.

It is assumed that students entering this course will have had little coverage of software engineering concepts previously, but have had two courses that give them a very good background in programming and basic computer science. The opposite assumptions are made for SE200.

It is suggested that a core subset of UML be taught, rather than trying to cover all features.

Rather than OCL, instructors can choose to introduce a different formal modeling technique.

Total hours of SEEK coverage: 34
CMP.ct (4 core hours of 20): Construction technologies
  CMP.ct.1: API design and use
  CMP.ct.2: Code reuse and libraries
  CMP.ct.3: Object-oriented run-time issues
FND.ef (3 core hours of 23): Engineering foundations for software
  FND.ef.1: Empirical methods and experimental techniques
  FND.ef.4: Systems development
  FND.ef.5: Engineering design
PRF.pr (1 core hour of 20): Professionalism
MAA.md (2 core hours of 19): Modeling
  MAA.md.1: Modeling principles
  MAA.md.2: Pre- & postconditions, invariants
  MAA.md.3: Introduction to mathematical models and specification languages
MAA.tm (1 core hour of 12): Types of models
MAA.rfd (1 core hour of 3): Requirements fundamentals
MAA.er (1 core hour of 4): Eliciting requirements
MAA.rsd (1 core hour of 6): Requirements specification & documentation
  MAA.rsd.3: Specification languages

MAA.rv (1 core hour of 3): Requirements validation
DES.con (2 core hours of 3): Software design concepts
DES.str (3 core hours of 6): Software design strategies
DES.ar (2 core hours of 9): Architectural design
DES.hci (1 core hour of 12): Human–computer interface design
DES.dd (2 core hours of 12): Detailed design
DES.nst (1 core hour of 3): Design notations and support tools
DES.ev (1 core hour of 3): Design evaluation
VAV.fnd (1 core hour of 5): V&V terminology and foundations
VAV.rev (1 core hour of 6): Reviews
VAV.tst (2 core hours of 21): Testing
VAV.par (1 core hour of 4): Problem analysis and reporting
PRO.imp (1 core hour of 10): Process implementation
MGT.con (1 core hour of 2): Management concepts

SE211 Software Construction

This course is part of Core Software Engineering Package I; it fits into slot A in the curriculum patterns.

Course Description:
General principles and techniques for disciplined low-level software design. BNF and basic theory of grammars and parsing. Use of parser generators. Basics of language and protocol design. Formal languages. State-transition and table-based software design. Formal methods for software construction. Techniques for handling concurrency and interprocess communication. Techniques for designing numerical software. Tools for model-driven construction. Introduction to middleware. Hot-spot analysis and performance tuning.
Prerequisite: (SE201 or SE200), CS103 and CS105.

Learning objectives:
Upon completion of this course, students will have the ability to:

- Apply a wide variety of software construction techniques and tools, including state-based and table-driven approaches to low-level software design

- Design simple languages and protocols suitable for a variety of applications

- Generate code for simple languages and protocols using suitable tools

- Create simple formal specifications of low-level software modules, check the validity of these specifications, and generate code from the specifications using appropriate tools

- Design simple concurrent software

- Analyze software to improve its efficiency, reliability, and maintainability

Suggested sequence of teaching modules:

1. Basics of formal languages; syntax and semantics, grammars, Backus Naur Form. Parsing; regular expressions and their relationship to state diagrams
2. Lexical analysis, tokens, more regular expressions and transition networks, principles of scanners
3. Using tools to generate scanners, applications of scanners, relation of scanners and compilers
4. Parsing concepts, parse trees, context-free grammars, LL Parsing
5. Overview of principles of programming languages, criteria for selecting programming languages and platforms
6. Tools for automating software design and construction, modeling system behavior with extended finite state machines
7. SDL
8. Representing concurrency and analyzing concurrent designs

Sample labs and assignments:

- Use of software engineering tools to create designs

- Use of parser generators to generate languages

Additional teaching considerations:
Students come to this course with a basic knowledge of finite state machines and concurrency; therefore, this course should cover more advanced material.

Total hours of SEEK coverage: 36
CMP.ct (10 core hours of 20): Construction technologies
  CMP.ct.6: Error handling, exception handling, and fault tolerance
  CMP.ct.7: State-based and table-driven construction techniques
  CMP.ct.8: Run-time configuration and internationalization
  CMP.ct.9: Grammar-based input processing
  CMP.ct.10: Concurrency primitives
  CMP.ct.11: Middleware
  CMP.ct.12: Construction methods for distributed software
  CMP.ct.14: Hot-spot analysis and performance tuning
CMP.tl (3 core hours of 4): Construction tools
CMP.fm (8 core hours of 8): Formal construction methods
FND.mf (11 core hours of 56): Mathematical foundations
  FND.mf.5 (1 core hour of 5): Graphs and trees
  FND.mf.7 (4 core hours of 4): Finite State Machines, regular expressions
  FND.mf.8 (4 core hours of 4): Grammars
  FND.mf.9 (2 core hours of 4): Numerical precision, accuracy, and errors
MAA.md (4 core hours of 19): Modeling

SE212 Software Engineering Approach to Human Computer Interaction

This course is part of Core Software Engineering Packages I and II; it fits into slot B in the curriculum patterns.

Course Description:
Psychological principles of human–computer interaction. Evaluation of user interfaces. Usability engineering. Task analysis, user-centered design, and prototyping. Conceptual models and metaphors. Software design rationale. Design of windows, menus, and commands. Voice and natural language I/O. Response time and feedback. Color, icons, and sound. Internationalization and localization. User interface architectures and APIs. Case studies and project.
Prerequisite: SE201 or SE200

Learning objectives:
Upon completion of this course, students will have the ability to:

- Evaluate software user interfaces using heuristic evaluation and user observation techniques

- Conduct simple formal experiments to evaluate usability hypotheses

- Apply user-centered design and usability engineering principles as they design a wide variety of software user interfaces

Suggested sequence of teaching modules:
1. Background to human–computer interaction. Underpinnings from psychology and cognitive science
2. More background. Evaluation techniques: heuristic evaluation
3. More evaluation techniques: Videotaped user testing, cognitive walkthroughs
4. Task analysis. User-centered design
5. Usability engineering processes, conducting experiments
6. Conceptual models and metaphors
7. Designing interfaces: Coding techniques using color, fonts, sound, animation, and so on
8. Designing interfaces: Screen layout, response time, feedback, error messages, and so on
9. Designing interfaces for special devices. Use of voice I/O
10. Designing interfaces: Internationalization, help systems, and so on. User interface software architectures
11. Expressing design rationale for user interface design

Sample labs and assignments:
- Evaluation of user interfaces using heuristic evaluation

- Evaluation of user interfaces using videotaped observation of users

- Paper prototyping of user interfaces, then discussing design options to arrive at a consensus design

- Writers-workshop for style, critiquing of prototypes presented by others

- Implementation of a system with a significant user interface component using a rapid prototyping environment

Additional teaching considerations:

- Some students naturally find it hard to relate to the needs of users, while others find the material in this course so intuitive that they are overconfident in this course. Students should be taught to obtain informed consent from users when involving them in the evaluation of user interfaces.

- A strategy that works well for this course is to teach process issues during one lecture each week, and design issues during another lecture each week, in effect running two courses in parallel.

- When task analysis is discussed, it should be compared to use case analysis.

- The writers' workshop format works well for teaching design in this course. Small groups of students present paper prototypes of their UI designs to the class. Other students in the class then express what they like about the designs. Next, the other students provide constructive criticism.

Total hours of SEEK coverage: 25
CMP.ct (1 core hour of 20): Construction technologies
  CMP.ct.8: Run-time configuration and internationalization
  CMP.tl.2: GUI builders
FND.ef (3 core hours of 23): Engineering foundations for software
PRF.psy (1 core hour of 5): Group dynamics/psychology
MAA.md (4 core hours of 19): Modeling
MAA.tm (1 core hour of 12): Types of models
  MAA.rfd.5: Analyzing quality
DES.hci (6 core hours of 12): Human–computer interface design
VAV.fnd (1 core hour of 5): V&V terminology and foundations
  VAV.fnd.4: Metrics and measurement
VAV.rev (1 core hour of 6): Reviews
  VAV.rev.3: Inspections
  VAV.tst.9: Testing across quality attributes
VAV.hct (6 core hours of 6): Human–computer user interface testing and evaluation
QUA.pda (1 core hour of 4): Product assurance
  QUA.pda.6: Assessment of product quality attributes

SE213 Design and Architecture of Large Software Systems

This course is part of Core Software Engineering Package II; it fits into slot A in the curriculum patterns.

Course Description:
Modeling and design of flexible software at the architectural level. Basics of model-driven architecture. Architectural styles and patterns. Middleware and application frameworks. Configurations and configuration management. Product lines. Design using commercial off-the-shelf (COTS) software.
Prerequisites: SE201 or SE200, and CS103

Learning objectives:
Upon completion of this course, students will have the ability to:

- Take requirements for simple systems and develop software architectures and high-level designs

- Use configuration management tools effectively and apply change management processes properly

- Design simple distributed software

- Design software using COTS components

- Apply a wide variety of frameworks and architectures in designing a wide variety of software

- Design and implement software using several different middleware technologies

Additional teaching considerations:
Students will be taking this before coverage of low-level design. Students, therefore, need tools and packages that allow them to implement their designs without much concern for low-level details.

Total hours of SEEK coverage: 28
MAA.md (5 core hours of 19): Modeling
MAA.tm (5 core hours of 12): Types of models
DES.str (2 core hours of 6): Software design strategies
DES.ar (5 core hours of 9): Architectural design
EVO.pro (3 core hours of 6): Evolution processes
  EVO.pro.1: Basic concepts of evolution and maintenance
  EVO.pro.2: Relationship between evolving entities
EVO.ac (2 core hours of 4): Evolution activities
MGT.con (1 core hour of 2): Management concepts
MGT.pp (1 core hour of 6): Project planning
MGT.cm (4 core hours of 5): Software configuration management

SE221 Software Testing

This course is part of Core Software Engineering Package II; it fits into slot C in the curriculum patterns.

Course Description:
Testing techniques and principles: Defects versus failures, equivalence classes, boundary testing. Types of defects. Black-box versus structural testing. Testing strategies: Unit testing, integration testing, profiling, test driven development. State-based testing, configuration testing, compatibility testing, Web site testing. Alpha, beta, and acceptance testing. Coverage criteria. Test instrumentation and tools. Developing test plans. Managing the testing process. Problem reporting, tracking, and analysis.
Prerequisites: SE201 or SE200

Learning objectives:
Upon completion of this course, students will have the ability to:

- Analyze requirements to determine appropriate testing strategies

- Design and implement comprehensive test plans

- Apply a wide variety of testing techniques in an effective and efficient manner

- Compute test coverage and yield according to a variety of criteria

- Use statistical techniques to evaluate the defect density and the likelihood of faults

- Conduct reviews and inspections

Additional teaching considerations:
This course is intended to be 95-percent testing, with deep coverage of a wide variety of testing techniques.

The course should build skill and experience in the student, preferably with production code.

Note that usability testing is covered in SE212.

Total hours of SEEK coverage: 23
MAA.rfd (1 core hour of 3): Requirements fundamentals
  MAA.rfd.4: Requirements characteristics
VAV.fnd (2 core hours of 5): V&V terminology and foundations
VAV.rev (1 core hour of 6): Reviews
VAV.tst (14 core hours of 21): Testing
  VAV.tst.2: Exception handling
VAV.par (3 core hours of 4): Problem analysis and reporting
QUA.pda (2 core hours of 4): Product assurance

SE311 Software Design and Architecture

This course is part of Core Software Engineering Package I; it fits into slot D in the curriculum patterns.

Course Description:
An in-depth look at software design. Continuation of the study of design patterns, frameworks, and architectures. Survey of current middleware architectures. Design of distributed systems using middleware. Component-based design. Measurement theory and appropriate use of metrics in design. Designing for qualities such as performance, safety, security, reusability, reliability, and so on. Measuring internal qualities and complexity of software. Evaluation and evolution of designs. Basics of software evolution, reengineering, and reverse engineering.
Prerequisites: SE211

Learning objectives:
Upon completion of this course, students will have the ability to:

- Apply a wide variety of design patterns, frameworks, and architectures in designing a wide variety of software

- Design and implement software using several different middleware technologies

- Use sound quality metrics as objectives for designs, and then measure and assess designs to ensure the objectives have been met

- Modify designs using sound change control approaches

- Use reverse engineering techniques to recapture the design of software

Suggested sequence of teaching modules:
1. In-depth study of design patterns, building on material learned previously
2. Application of design patterns to several example applications
3. In-depth study of middleware architectures including COM, Corba, and .Net
4. Extensive case studies of real designs
5. Basics of software metrics; measuring software qualities
6. Reengineering and reverse-engineering techniques

Sample labs and assignments:

- Building a significant project using one or more well-known middleware architectures

Additional teaching considerations:
Students will already have a knowledge of some basic design patterns; this course will cover current pattern catalogs in significant detail, not just limited to the classic "Gang of Four" patterns.

Total hours of SEEK coverage: 33
CMP.ct (3 core hours of 20): Construction technologies
  CMP.ct.11: Middleware
  CMP.ct.12: Construction methods for distributed software
  CMP.ct.13: Constructing heterogeneous systems
MAA.md (4 core hours of 19): Modeling
MAA.tm.3: Structure modeling
DES.str (2 core hours of 6): Software design strategies
DES.ar (5 core hours of 9): Architectural design
DES.dd (8 core hours of 12): Detailed design
DES.nst (1 core hour of 3): Design notations and support tools
DES.ev (1 core hour of 3): Design evaluation
EVO.pro (5 core hours of 6): Evolution processes
EVO.ac (4 core hours of 4): Evolution activities

SE312 Low-Level Design of Software

This course is part of Core Software Engineering Package II; it fits into slot D in the curriculum patterns.

Course Description:

Detailed software design and construction in depth. In-depth coverage of design patterns and refactoring. Introduction to formal approaches to design. Analysis of designs based on internal quality criteria. Performance and maintainability improvement. Reverse engineering. Disciplined approaches to design change.
Prerequisite: SE213

Learning objectives:
Upon completion of this course, students will have the ability to:

- Apply a wide variety of software construction techniques and tools, including state-based and table-driven approaches to low-level design of software

- Use a wide variety of design patterns in the design of software

- Perform object-oriented design and programming with a high level of proficiency

- Analyze software to improve its efficiency, reliability, and maintainability

- Modify designs using sound change-control approaches

- Use reverse-engineering techniques to recapture the design of software

Additional teaching considerations:
Students will have already learned a lot about high-level design and architecture. This course covers low-level details.

Total hours of SEEK coverage: 26
CMP.ct (13 core hours of 20): Construction technologies
CMP.tl (3 core hours of 4): Construction tools
CMP.fm (2 core hours of 8): Formal construction methods
MAA.tm (2 core hours of 12): Types of models
DES.dd (5 core hours of 12): Detailed design
EVO.ac (1 core hour of 4): Evolution activities

SE313 Formal Methods in Software Engineering

This course is part of Core Software Engineering Package II; it fits into slot F in the curriculum patterns.

Course Description:
Review of mathematical foundations for formal methods. Formal languages and techniques for specification and design, including specifying syntax using grammars and finite state machines. Analysis and verification of specifications and designs. Use of assertions and proofs. Automated program and design transformation.
Prerequisite: SE312

Learning objectives:
Upon completion of this course, students will have the ability to:

- Create mathematically precise specifications and designs using languages such as OCL, Z, and so on

- Analyze the properties of formal specifications and designs

- Use tools to transform specifications and designs

Total hours of SEEK coverage: 34
CMP.fm (6 core hours of 8): Formal construction methods
FND.mf (13 core hours of 56): Mathematical foundations
  FND.mf.5 (1 core hour of 5): Graphs and trees
  FND.mf.7 (4 core hours of 4): Finite state machines, regular expressions
  FND.mf.8 (4 core hours of 4): Grammars
  FND.mf.9 (4 core hours of 4): Numerical precision, accuracy, and errors
MAA.md (3 core hours of 19): Modeling
  MAA.md.3: Introduction to mathematical models and specification languages
MAA.tm (2 core hours of 12): Types of models
MAA.tm.2: Behavioral modeling
MAA.rsd (3 core hours of 6): Requirements specification and documentation
  MAA.rsd.3: Specification languages
MAA.rv (1 core hour of 3): Requirements validation
DES.dd (3 core hours of 12): Detailed design
DES.nst (1 core hour of 3): Design notations and support tools
  DES.nst.6: Formal design analysis
DES.ev (1 core hour of 3): Design evaluation
  DES.ev.2: Evaluation techniques
EVO.ac (1 core hour of 4): Evolution activities
  EVO.ac.6: Refactoring
  EVO.ac.7: Program transformation

SE321 Software Quality Assurance and Testing

This course is part of Core Software Engineering Package I; it fits into slot C in the curriculum patterns.

Course Description:
Quality: How to assure it and verify it, and the need for a culture of quality. Avoidance of errors and other quality problems. Inspections and reviews. Testing, verification and validation techniques. Process assurance versus product assurance. Quality process standards. Product and process assurance. Problem analysis and reporting. Statistical approaches to quality control.
Prerequisite: SE201 or SE200

Learning objectives:
Upon completion of this course, students will have the ability to:

- Conduct effective and efficient inspections

- Design and implement comprehensive test plans

- Apply a wide variety of testing techniques in an effective and efficient manner

- Compute test coverage and yield, according to a variety of criteria

- Use statistical techniques to evaluate the defect density and the likelihood of faults

- Assess a software process to evaluate how effective it is at promoting quality

Suggested sequence of teaching modules:
1. Introduction to software quality assurance
2. Inspections and reviews
3. Principles of software validation
4. Software verification
5. Software testing
6. Specification-based test construction techniques
7. White-box and grey-box testing
8. Control-flow-oriented test construction techniques
9. Dataflow-oriented test construction techniques
10. Cleanroom approach to quality assurance
11. Software process certification

Sample labs and assignments:
- Use of automated testing tools

- Testing of a wide variety of software

- Application of a wide variety of testing techniques

- Inspecting of software in teams, comparison and analysis of results

Additional teaching considerations:
User interface testing with end-users is covered in SE212, so it should not be covered here. However, the use of test harnesses that work through the user interface is an appropriate topic.

The reason why testing is to be emphasized so much is not that other techniques are less important, but because many other techniques (for example, inspections) can more easily be learned on the job, whereas testing material tends to require course-based learning to be mastered properly.

Total hours of SEEK coverage: 37
FND.mf (2 core hours of 56): Mathematical foundations
   FND.mf.9 (2 core hours of 4): Numerical precision, accuracy, and errors
VAV.fnd (2 core hours of 5): V&V terminology and foundations
VAV.rev (1 core hour of 6): Reviews
VAV.tst (14 core hours of 21): Testing
VAV.par (3 core hours of 4): Problem analysis and reporting
PRO.con (1 core hour of 3): Process concepts
QUA.cc (1 core hour of 2): Software quality concepts and culture
QUA.std (2 core hours of 2): Software quality standards
QUA.pro (4 core hours of 4): Software quality processes
QUA.pca (4 core hours of 4): Process assurance
QUA.pda (3 core hours of 4): Product assurance

SE322 Software Requirements Analysis

This course is part of Core Software Engineering Package I; it fits into slot E in the curriculum patterns.

Course Description:
Domain engineering. Techniques for discovering and eliciting requirements. Languages and models for representing requirements. Analysis and validation techniques, including need, goal, and use-case analysis. Requirements in the context of system engineering. Specifying and measuring external qualities: performance, reliability, availability, safety, security, and so on. Specifying and analyzing requirements for various types of systems: embedded systems, consumer systems, Web-based systems, business systems, and systems for scientists and other engineers. Resolving feature interactions. Requirements documentation standards. Traceability. Human factors. Requirements in the context of agile processes. Requirements management: Handling requirements changes.
Prerequisites: SE201 or SE200

Learning objectives:
Upon completion of this course, students will have the ability to:

- Discover or elicit requirements using a variety of techniques

- Organize and prioritize requirements

- Apply analysis techniques such as needs analysis, goal analysis, and use-case analysis

- Validate requirements according to criteria such as feasibility, clarity, and freedom from ambiguity

- Represent functional and nonfunctional requirements for different types of systems using formal and informal techniques

- Specify and measure quality attributes

- Negotiate among different stakeholders to agree on a set of requirements

- Detect and resolve feature interactions

Suggested sequence of teaching modules:
1. Basics of software requirements engineering
2. Requirements engineering process: requirements elicitation, specification, analysis, and management
3. Types of requirements: functional, nonfunctional, quality attributes
4. Requirements elicitation: identifying needs, goals, and requirements. Customers and other stakeholders. Interviews and observations
5. Requirements specification: textual and graphical notations and languages (UML, user requirements notation). Techniques to write high-quality requirements. Documentation standards
6. Requirements analysis: inspection, validation, completeness, detection of conflicts and inconsistencies. Feature interaction analysis and resolution
7. Goal- and use-case-oriented modeling, prototyping, and analysis techniques

8. Requirements for typical systems: embedded systems, consumer systems, Web-based systems, business systems, systems for scientists and other engineers
9. Requirements management: traceability, priorities, changes, baselines, and tool support
10. Requirements negotiation and risk management
11. Integrating requirements analysis and software processes (including agile ones)

Sample labs and assignments:

- Writing good requirements

- Analysis of a wide variety of existing software systems: Measuring qualities, and reverse-engineering requirements

- Interviewing users and translating the results into prototypes iteratively

- Use of tools for managing requirements

- Modeling, prototyping, and analyzing requirements with UML/URN tools

- Resolving feature interactions

Additional teaching considerations:
Those teaching this course will have to put special effort into motivating students who prefer the technical and programming side of software engineering. It would be useful to give examples where bad requirements have led to disasters (economic or physical). Interaction with real or simulated customers would also be beneficial.

Total hours of SEEK coverage: 18
MAA.tm (9 core hours of 12): Types of models
MAA.rfd (1 core hour of 3): Requirements fundamentals
MAA.er (2 core hours of 4): Eliciting requirements
MAA.rsd (4 core hours of 6): Requirements specification and documentation
MAA.rv (1 core hour of 3): Requirements validation
MAA.rfd.6 (1 core hour of 3): Requirements management

SE323 Software Project Management

This course is part of Core Software Engineering Package I; it fits into slot F in the curriculum patterns.

Course Description:
Project planning, cost estimation, and scheduling. Project management tools. Factors influencing productivity and success. Productivity metrics. Analysis of options and risks. Planning for change. Management of expectations. Release and configuration management. Software process standards and process implementation. Software contracts and intellectual property. Approaches to maintenance and long-term software development. Case studies of real industrial projects.
Prerequisites: SE321 and SE322

Learning objectives:
Upon completion of this course, students will have the ability to:

- Develop a comprehensive project plan for a significant development effort

- Apply management techniques to projects that follow agile methodologies, as well as methodologies involve larger-scale iterations or releases

- Effectively estimate costs for a project using several different techniques

- Apply function point measurement techniques

- Measure project progress, productivity and other aspects of the software process

- Apply earned-value analysis techniques

- Perform risk management, dynamically adjusting project plans

- Use configuration management tools effectively, and apply change management processes properly

- Draft and evaluate basic software licenses, contracts, and intellectual property agreements, while recognizing the necessity of involving legal expertise

- Use standards in project management, including ISO 10006 (project management quality) and ISO 12207 (software development process) along with the SEI's CMM model

Suggested sequence of teaching modules:
1. Basic concepts of project management
2. Managing requirements
3. Software life cycles
4. Software estimation
5. The project plan
6. Monitoring the project
7. Risk analysis
8. Managing quality
9. People problems

Sample labs and assignments:

- Use a commercial project management tool to assist with all aspects of software project management, including creation of Gantt, PERT, and Earned Value charts

- Make cost estimates for a small system using a variety of techniques

- Developing a project plan for a significant system

- Writing a configuration management plan

- Using change-control and configuration-management tools

- Evaluating a software contract or license

Total hours of SEEK coverage: 26
MAA.mgt (2 core hours of 3): Requirements management
PRO.con (2 core hours of 3): Process concepts
PRO.imp (9 core hours of 10): Process implementation
MGT.con (1 core hour of 2): Management concepts

MGT.pp (3 core hours of 6): Project planning
MGT.per (1 core hour of 2): Project personnel and organization
MGT.ctl (4 core hours of 4): Project control
MGT.cm (4 core hours of 5): Software configuration management

SE324 Software Process and Management

This course is part of Core Software Engineering Package II; it fits into slot E in the curriculum patterns.

Course Description:
Software processes: standards, implementation, and assurance. Project management with a focus on requirements management and long-term evolution: Eliciting and prioritizing requirements, cost estimation, planning and tracking projects, risk analysis, project control, change management.
Prerequisites: SE201 or SE200, plus at least two additional software engineering courses at the 2-level or higher.

Learning objectives:
Upon completion of this course, students will have the ability to:

- Elicit requirements using a variety of techniques

- Organize and prioritize requirements

- Design processes suitable for different types of project

- Assess a software process to evaluate how effective it promotes quality

- Develop a comprehensive project plan for a significant development effort

- Measure project progress, productivity, and other aspects of the software process

- Effectively estimate costs for development and evolution of a system using several different techniques

- Perform risk management, dynamically adjusting project plans

- Use standards for quality, process and project management

- Perform root cause analysis and work toward continual improvement of process

Total hours of SEEK coverage: 39
MAA.er (2 core hours of 4): Eliciting requirements
MAA.rsd (1 core hour of 6): Requirements specification and documentation
MAA.rfd.6 (3 core hours of 3): Requirements management
EVO.pro (2 core hours of 6): Evolution processes
   EVO.pro.3: Models of software evolution
   EVO.pro.4: Cost models of evolution
PRO.con (3 core hours of 3): Process concepts
PRO.imp (9 core hours of 10): Process implementation
QUA.cc (1 core hour of 2): Software quality concepts and culture

QUA.std (2 core hours of 2): Software quality standards
QUA.pro (4 core hours of 4): Software quality processes
QUA.pca (4 core hours of 4): Process assurance
QUA.pda (1 core hour of 4): Product assurance
MGT.pp (2 core hours of 6): Project planning
MGT.per (1 core hour of 2): Project personnel and organization
MGT.ctl (4 core hours of 4): Project control

Capstone project course

SE400 Software Engineering Capstone Project

The capstone project has been part of an engineering curriculum since the days when the stone mason was asked to carve a decorated "capstone" to signal his achievement of mastery of his craft.

Course Description:
Development of significant software system, employing knowledge gained from courses throughout the program. Includes development of requirements, design, implementation, and quality assurance. Students can follow any suitable process model, must pay attention to quality issues, and must manage the project themselves, following all appropriate project-management techniques. Success of the project is determined in large part by whether students have adequately solved their customer's problem.
Prerequisites: Completion of the level-3 courses in one of the curriculum patterns.

Sample deliverables:
Students should be expected to deliver one or several iterations of a software system, along with all artifacts appropriate to the process model they are using. These would likely include a project plan (perhaps updated regularly, and containing cost estimations, risk analysis, division of the work into tasks, and so on), requirements (including use cases), architectural and design documents, test plans, source code, and installable system.

Additional teaching considerations:

- It is anticipated that this course will not have formal lectures, although students would be expected to attend progress presentations by other groups.

- It is suggested that students be required to have a "customer" for whom they are developing their software. This could be a company, a professor, or several people selected as representing people in the potential market. The objective of the project would be to solve the customer's problem, and the customer would therefore assist the instructor in evaluating the work.

- It is strongly suggested that students work in groups of at least two, and preferably three or four, on their capstone project. Strategies must be developed to handle situations where the contribution of team members is unequal.

- Some institutions may wish to divide this course into two parts, one per semester for example. In such a case, it is suggested, however, that if students do not finish the project (that is, the second of the two courses), they should have to start from the first course again.

Total hours of SEEK coverage: 28

This material represents SEEK units that must be practiced in all projects. Beyond this, different projects will exercise skills in different areas of SEEK.

CMP.ct (1 core hour of 20): Construction technologies
PRF.psy (1 core hour of 5): Group dynamics/psychology
PRF.com (2 core hours of 10): Communications skills
PRF.pr (2 core hours of 20): Professionalism
MAA.tm (1 core hour of 12): Types of models
MAA.er (1 core hour of 4): Eliciting requirements
MAA.rsd (1 core hour of 6): Requirements specification and documentation
MAA.rv (1 core hour of 3): Requirements validation
DES.str (1 core hour of 6): Software design strategies
DES.ar (2 core hours of 9): Architectural design
DES.hci (2 core hours of 12): Human–computer interface design
DES.dd (2 core hours of 12): Detailed design
DES.nst (1 core hour of 3): Design notations and support tools
DES.ev (1 core hour of 3): Design evaluation
VAV.rev (2 core hours of 6): Reviews
VAV.tst (3 core hours of 21): Testing
MGT.pp (2 core hours of 6): Project planning
MGT.per (1 core hour of 2): Project personnel and organization
MGT.cm (1 core hour of 5): Software configuration management

Appendix B: Contributors and Reviewers

Education Knowledge Area volunteers

Jonathan D. Addelston, UpStart Systems, US
Roger Alexander, Colorado State University, US
Niniek Angkasaputra, Fraunhofer Institute of Experimental Software Engineering, Germany
Mark A. Ardis, Rose-Hulman University, US
Jocelyn Armarego, Murdoch University, Australia
Doug Baldwin, The State University of New York, Geneseo, US
Earl Beede, Construx, US
Fawsy Bendeck, University of Kaiserslautern, Germany
Mordechai Ben-Menachem, Ben-Gurion University, Israel
Robert Burnett, consultant, Brazil
Kai Chang, Auburn University, US
Jason Chen, National Central University, Taiwan
Cynthia Cicalese, Marymount University, US
Tony (Anthony) Cowling, University of Sheffield, UK
David Dampier, Mississippi State University, US
Mel Damodaran, University of Houston, US
Onur Demirors, Middle East Technical University, Turkey
Vladan Devedzic, University of Belgrade, Yugoslavia
Oscar Dieste, University of Alfonso X El Sabio, Spain
Dick Fairley, Oregon Graduate Institute, US
Mohamed E. Fayad, University of Nebraska, Lincoln, US
Orit Hazzan, Israel Institute of Technology, Israel
Bill Hefley, Carnegie Mellon University, US
Peter Henderson, Butler University, US
Joel Henry, University of Montana, US
Jens Jahnke, University of Victoria, Canada
Stanislaw Jarzabek, National University of Singapore, Singapore
Natalia Juristo, Universidad Politecnica of Madrid, Spain
Umit Karakas, consultant, Turkey
Atchutarao Killamsetty, JENS SpinNet, Japan
Haim Kilov, Financial Systems Architects, US
Moshe Krieger, University of Ottawa, Canada
Hareton Leung, Hong Kong Polytechnic University, Hong Kong
Marta Lopez, Fraunhofer Institute of Experimental Software Engineering, Germany
Mike Lutz, Rochester Institute of Technology, US
Paul E. MacNeil, Mercer University, US
Mike McCracken, Georgia Institute of Technology, US
James McDonald, Monmouth University, US
Emilia Mendes, University of Auckland, New Zealand
Luisa Mich, University of Trento, Italy
Ana Moreno, Universidad Politecnica of Madrid, Spain
Traian Muntean, University of Marseilles, France
Keith Olson, Utah Valley State College, US

Michael Oudshoorn, University of Adelaide, Australia
Dietmar Pfahl, Fraunhofer Institute of Experimental Software Engineering, Germany
Mario Piattini, University of Castilla-La Mancha, Spain
Francis Pinheiro, University of Brazil, Brazil
Valentina Plekhanova, University of Sunderland, UK
Hossein Saiedian, University of Kansas, US
Stephen C. Schwarm, EMC, US
Peraphon Sophatsathit, Chulalongkorn University, Thailand
Jennifer S. Stuart, Construx, US
Linda T. Taylor, Taylor & Zeno Systems, US
Richard Thayer, California State University, Sacramento, US
Jim Tomayko, Carnegie Melon University, US
Massood Towhidnejad, Embry-Riddle University, US
Joseph E. Urban, Arizona State University, US
Arie van Deursen, National Research Institute for Mathematics & Computer Science, Netherlands
Sira Vegas, University of Madrid, Spain
Bimlesh Wadhwa, National University of Singapore, Singapore
Yingxu Wang, University of Calgary, Canada
Mary Jane Willshire, University of Portland, US
Mansour Zand, University of Nebraska, Omaha, US
Jianhan Zhu, University of Ulster, UK

SE2004 SEEK workshop attendees

Earl Beede, Construx, US
Pierre Bourque, University of Quebec, Canada
David Budgen, Keele University, UK
Kai Chang, Auburn University, US
Jorge L. Díaz-Herrera, Rochester Institute of Technology, US
Frank Driscoll, Mitre Corporation, US
Steve Easterbrook, University of Toronto, Canada
Dick Fairley, Oregon Graduate Institute, US
Peter Henderson, Butler University, US
Thomas B. Hilburn, Embry-Riddle University, US
Tom Horton, University of Virginia, US
Cem Kaner, Florida Institute of Technology, US
Haim Kilov, Financial Systems Architects, US
Gideon Kornblum, Getronics, Netherlands
Rich LeBlanc, Georgia Institute of Technology, US
Timothy C. Lethbridge, University of Ottawa, Canada
Bill Marion, Valparaiso University, US
Yoshihiro Matsumoto, Musashi Institute of Technology, Japan
Mike McCracken, Georgia Institute of Technology, US
Andrew McGettrick, University of Strathclyde, UK
Susan Mengel, Texas Tech University, US
Traian Muntean, University of Marseilles, France

Keith Olson, Utah Valley State College, US
Allen Parrish, University of Alabama, US
Ann Sobel, Miami University, US
Jenny Stuart, Construx, US
Linda T. Taylor, Taylor & Zeno Systems, US
Barrie Thompson, University of Sunderland, UK
Richard Upchurch, University of Massachusetts, US
Frank H. Young, Rose-Hulman University, US

SEEK internal reviewers

Barry Boehm, University of Southern California, US
Kai H. Chang, Auburn University, US
Jason Jen-Yen Chen, National Central University, Taiwan
Tony Cowling, University of Sheffield, UK
Vladan Devedzic, University of Belgrade, Yugoslavia
Laura Dillon, Michigan State University, US
Dennis J. Frailey, Raytheon, US
Peter Henderson, Butler University, US
Watts Humphrey, Software Engineering Institute, US
Haim Kilov, Financial Systems Architects, US
Hareton Leung, Hong Kong Polytechnic University, Hong Kong
Yoshihiro Matsumoto, Information Processing Society, Japan
Bertrand Meyer, ETH, Zurich
Luisa Mich, University of Trento, Italy
James W. Moore, Mitre Corporation, US
Hausi Muller, University of Victoria, Canada
Peter G. Neuman, SRI International, US
David Notkin, University of Washington, US
Dietmar Pfahl, Fraunhofer Institute of Experimental Software Engineering, Germany
Mary Shaw, Carnegie Mellon University, US
Ian Sommerville, Lancaster University, UK
Peraphon Sophatsathit, Chulalongkorn University, Thailand
Steve Tockey, Construx Software, US
Massood Towhidnejad, Embry-Riddle University, US
Leonard Tripp, Boeing Shared Services, US

SEEK external reviewers

James P. Alstad, Hughes Space and Communications Company, US
Niniek Angkasaputra, Fraunhofer Institute for Experimental SE, Germany
Hernan Astudillo, Financial Systems Architects, US
Donald J. Bagert, Rose-Hulman Institute of Technology, US
Mario R. Barbacci, Software Engineering Institute, US
Ilia Bider, IbisSoft AB, Sweden
Grady Booch, Rational Corp, US
Jurgen Borstler, Umeå University, Sweden

Pierre Bourque, Ecole de Technologie Superieure, Montreal, Canada
David Budgen, Keele University, UK
Joe Clifton, University of Wisconsin, Platteville, US
Kendra Cooper, University of Texas at Dallas, US
Tony Cowling, University of Sheffield, UK
Vladan Devedzic, University of Belgrade, Yugoslavia
Rick Duley, Edith Cowan University, Australia
Robert Dupuis, Universite de Quebec à Montreal, Canada
Juan Garbajosa, Universidad Politecnica de Madrid, Spain
Robert L. Glass, Indiana University, US
Orit Hazzan, Technion—Israel Institute of Technology, Israel
Hui Huang, National Institute of Standards and Technology, US
IFIP Working Group 2.9
Joseph Kasser, University of South Australia
Khaled Khan, University of Western Sydney, Australia
Peter Knoke, University of Alaska, Fairbanks, US
Gideon Kornblum, CManagement bv, Netherlands
Claude Laporte, Ecole de Technologie Superieure, Montreal, Canada
Ansik Lee, Texas Instruments, US
Hareton Leung, Hong Kong Polytechnic University, Hong Kong
Grace Lewis, Software Engineering Institute, US
Michael Lutz, Rochester Institute of Technology, US
Andrew Malton, University of Waterloo, Canada
Nikolai Mansurov, KLOCwork Inc., Ottawa, Canada
Esperanza Marcos, Rey Juan Carlos University, Spain
Pat Martin, Florida Institute of Technology, US
Kenneth L. Modesitt, Indiana University—Purdue University Fort Wayne, US
Ibrahim Mohamed, Universiti Kebangsaan, Malaysia
James Moore, Mitre Corporation, US
Keith Paton, independent consultant, Montreal, Canada
Pedagogy Focus Group volunteers
Valentina Plekhanova, University of Sunderland, UK
Steve Roach, University of Texas at El Paso, US
Francois Robert, Ecole de Technologie Superieure, Montreal, Canada
Robert C. Seacord, Software Engineering Institute, US
Peraphon Sophatsathit, Chulalongkorn University, Thailand
Witold Suryn, Ecole de Technologie Superieure, Montreal, Canada
Sylvie Trudel, Ecole de Technologie Superieure, Montreal, Canada
Hans van Vliet, Vrije Universiteit Amsterdam, Netherlands
Frank H. Young, Rose-Hulman Institute of Technology, US
Zdzislaw Zurakowski, Institute of Power Systems Automation, Poland

SE2004 Pedagogy volunteers

Jonathan Addelston, US
Donald Bagert, Rose-Hulman Institute of Technology, US
Jürgen Börstler, Umea Universitet, Sweden
David Budgen, Keele University, UK
Joe Clifton, University of Wisconsin, Plattsburgh, US
Kendra Cooper, University of Texas, Dallas, US
Vladan Devedzic, University of Belgrade, Yugoslavia
Rick Duley, Perth, Western Australia
Garth Glynn, University of Brighton, UK
Elizabeth Hawthorne, Union County College, US
Orit Hazzan, Technion, Israel
Justo Hidalgo, Universidad Antonio de Nebrija, Spain
M. Umit Karakas, Turkey
Khaled Khan, University of Western Sydney, Australia
Yoshihiro Matsumoto, ASTEM Research Institute of Kyoto, Japan
Pat McGee, Florida Institute of Technology, US
Andrew McGettrick, University of Strathclyde, UK
Bruce Maxim, University of Michigan, US
Ken Modesitt, Indiana University—Purdue University Fort Wayne, US
Steve Roach, University of Texas at El Paso, US
Anthony Ruocco, Roger Williams University, US
Peraphon Sophatsathit, Chulalongkorn University, Thailand
Barrie Thompson, University of Sunderland, UK
Yingxu Wang, University of Calgary, Canada
Frank H. Young, Rose-Hulman Institute of Technology, US

SE2004 draft reviewers

Robert L. Ashenhurst, Graduate School of Business, University of Chicago, US
Donald Bagert, Rose-Hulman Institute of Technology, US
Bruce H. Barnes, US
Larry Bernstein, Stevens Institute of Technology—Computer Science, US
Jürgen Börstler, Umea Universitet, Sweden
Vincent Chiew, University of Calgary/Axis Cogni-Solve Ltd., Canada
Tony Cowling, University of Sheffield, UK
Deepak Dahiya, Institute for Integrated Learning in Management, India
Wes Doonan, Movaz Networks, US
Rick Duley, Murdoch University, Australia
David Parnas, University of Limerick, Ireland
Helen M Edwards, University of Sunderland, UK
Matthias Felleisen, Northeastern University, US
Maurizio Fenati, Micron Technology Italia, Italy
Robert L. Glass, Computing Trends, US
Garth Glynn, University of Brighton, UK
William Griswold, University of California, San Diego, US

Duncan Hall, EDS CPEng, IntPE, MIPENZ, SMIEEE, ACM, New Zealand
Rob Hasker, University of Wisconsin, Platteville, US
Bill Hefley, Carnegie Mellon University, US
Jonathan Hodgson, Saint Joseph's University, US
Vladan Jovanovic, Georgia Southern University, US
Cem Kaner, Florida Institute of Technology, US
Pete Knoke, University of Alaska, Fairbanks, US
Hareton Leung, Hong Kong Polytechnic University, China
Tim H. Lin, ECE Department, Cal Poly Pomona, US
Michael Lutz, Rochester Institute of Technology, US
Dino Mandrioli, Politecnico di Milano, Italy
Luisa Mich, University of Trento, Italy
Ivan Mistrik, Fraunhofer IPSI, Germany
James Moore, Mitre Corporation, US
Ana Moreno, Universidad Politecnica de Madrid, Spain
Carl J. Mueller, US
Ricardo Colomo Palacios, Universidad Carlos III, Spain
Volodymyr Pavlov, eLine Software, Ukraine
Kai Qian, Southern Polytechnic State University, US
David Rine, George Mason University, US
Andrey A.Terekhov, Microsoft, US
John Walz, Software Quality Consultant, US
Michael Wing, Vandyke Software, US
Tony Wasserman, Software Methods and Tools, US

Attendees at the SE2004 workshop held at the Conference on Software Engineering Education and Training (CSEE&T 2002), Covington, Kentucky, February 25, 2002

"Requirements" group
Keith B Olsen, Utah Valley State College, US
Massood Towhidnejad, Embry-Riddle University, US
Wing Lam, Institute of Systems Science, US
Dennis Frailey, Raytheon Corporation, US
Lynda Thomas, University of Wales, UK

"Design" group
Norm Cregger, Central Michigan University, US
Richard Conn, Lockheed Martin, US
John W. Fendrich, Bradley University, US
Heikki Saoslamoinen, University of Jyvaskyla, Finland
Jim McDonald, Monmouth University, US
David Umphress, Auburn University, US

"Quality" group
Elizabeth Hawthorne, ACM TYC & Union County College, US
Michael Ryan, Dublin City University, Ireland
Ellen Walker

Dermot Shinners-Kennedy
Jocelyn Armarego, Murdoch University, US
Ian Newman, Loughborough University, UK

"Process" group
Orit Hazzan, Technion—Israel Institute of Technology
Jim Kiper, Miami University, US
Cindy Tanur
Dick Lytle, Towson University, US
Rob Hasker, University of Wisconsin, Platteville, US
Peter Henderson, Butler University, US
Nabeel Al-Fayoumi, Ministry of Information & Communication Technology, Jordan

Workshop organizers
Barrie Thompson, University of Sunderland, UK
Helen Edwards, University of Sunderland, UK

SE2004 Steering Committee members
Jorge L. Díaz-Herrera, Rochester Institute of Technology, US
Thomas B. Hilburn, Embry-Riddle Aeronautical University, US
Rich LeBlanc, Georgia Institute of Technology, US
Ann Sobel, Miami University, US

Attendees at the International Summit on Software Engineering Education (SSEE 2002) colocated with ICSE 2002, May 21, 2002

Paulo Alencar, University of Waterloo, Canada
Joanne Atlee, University of Waterloo, Canada
Pierre Bourque, University of Quebec, Canada
Tony (Anthony) Cowling, University of Sheffield, UK
P. Devanbu, University of California, US
Helen M. Edwards, University of Sunderland, UK
Martin Griss, Hewlett-Packard, US
Thomas B. Hilburn, Embry-Riddle University, US
Bob Kossler, University of Utah, US
Timothy C. Lethbridge, University of Ottawa, Canada
Meir (Manny) Lehman, Imperial College, UK
Sam Redwine, James Madison University, US
Karl Reed, Bond University, Australia
Ken Robinson, University of New South Wales, Australia
J. Barrie Thompson, University of Sunderland, UK
Debora Weber-Wulff, Virtvelle Fachhochschule, Germany

Attendees at the SE2004 workshop held at the Conference on Software Engineering Education and Training (CSEE&T 2003), Madrid, March 20, 2003

Jocelyn Armarego, Murdoch University, Australia

Donald J. Bagert, Rose-Hulman Institute of Technology, US
Pere Botella, Technical University of Catalonia, Barcelona, Spain
Pierre Bourque, University of Quebec, Canada
David Budgen, Keele University, UK
John Cooke, University of Sarkatchen, Canada
Tony (Anthony) Cowling, University of Sheffield, UK
Jose Javier Dolado, University of the Basque Country, Spain
Gilles Y. Delisle, University of Ottawa, Canada
Robert Dupuis, Universite de Quebec à Monteal, Canada
Helen M. Edwards, University of Sunderland, UK
Juan Garbajosa, Technical University of Madrid, Spain
Orit Hazzan, Israel Institute of Technology, Israel
Tusto N. Hidaleo, University of Nebrua, Spain
Thomas B. Hilburn, Embry-Riddle University, US
Greg Hislop, Drexel University, US
Rich LeBlanc, Georgia Institute of Technology, US
Timothy C. Lethbridge, University of Ottawa, Canada
Keith Mansfield, Addison Wesley/Pearson Education, US
Mike Murphy, Southern Polytechnic State university, US
Faye Navabi, Arizona State University, US
Bill Poole, Seattle University, US
Stephen Seidman, New Jersey Institute of Technology, US
Mark Sebern, Milwaukee School of Engineering, US
J. Barrie Thompson, University of Sunderland, UK

Registrants/attendees at the Second International Summit on Software Engineering Education (SSEE II) colocated with ICSE 2003, May 5, 2003

James Andrews, University of Western Ontario, Canada
Joanne Atlee, University of Waterloo, Canada
Duncan Clarke, University of South Carolina, US
Oliver Creighton, Technische Universitat Munchen, Germany
Geoff Dromey, Griffith University, Australia
Amnon Eden, University of Essex, UK
Helen M. Edwards, University of Sunderland, UK
Keith Frampton, RMIT University, Australia
Keith Gallager, Loyola College, US
Stanislav Jarzabek, National University of Singapore
Cem Kaner, Florida Tech, US
Philip Koopman, Carnegie Mellon University, US
Rich LeBlank, Georgia Institute of Technology, US
Timothy C. Lethbridge, University of Ottawa, Canada
Pat McGee, Florida Tech, US
James McKim, Rensselaer, US
Everald Mills, Seattle University, US
Hausi Muller, University of Victoria, Canada
Arturo Sanchez, University of North Florida, US

Mary Shaw, Carnegie Mellon University, US
Andrew Simpson, Oxford University, UK
J. Barrie Thompson, University of Sunderland, UK
Kevin Twitchell, Brigham Young University, US

Index

A

ACM · ii, 1, 76
   Education Board · 3
AIS · *See* Association for Information
   Systems
AITP · *See* Association of Information
   Technology Professionals
associate-degree · 69
Association for Computing Machinery · 1,
   75, 81, 82
Association for Information Systems · 2
Association of Information Technology
   Professionals · 2

B

Bloom's attributes · 20
Bloom's taxonomy · 17, 20

C

Capstone project · 15
CC2001 Computer Science volume · 1
CC2001 Task Force · *See* task force
CCCS · 1, 3, 4, 11, 21, 22, 23, 47, 83, 84,
   87, 88, 89, 90, 91, 92, 97, 99. *See* CC2001
community colleges · 69
computer engineering · 1, 2, 73
Computer Society of the IEEE · 1
computing · 1, 5, 13, 23, 40, 54, 75, 83, 84,
   85, 87, 90, 93, 96, 97, 98, 101
computing disciplines · ii
computing essentials · 21
Conference on Software Engineering
   Education & Training · 2, 3, 11, 65, 79,
   80
Core Software Engineering Sequences ·
   54
CSEE&T · 65, 76, 78. *See* Conference on
   Software Engineering Education and
   Training

curricula · 47
curriculum · 1
   Australian pattern · 64
   coding scheme · 48
   components · 13
   coverage · 37
   CS-first approach · 50, 52
   designers and instructors · 36
   Engineering nature · 39
   guidelines · 36
   infrastructure · 71
   internationalism · 14
   introductory sequence · 49
   Israel pattern · 64
   Japanese pattern · 63
   learning objectives · 37
   Non-SEEK courses · 58
   North American universities · 60
   outcomes · 2, 14, 37
   patterns · 59
   principles · 13
   SE-first approach · 50, 51
curriculum task force · 1

D

design · 8
   domain-specific · 9
   engineering design · 8, 15, 23
domains · 39

E

education knowledge areas · *See* knowledge
   areas

F

faculty · *See* Software Engineering: faculty
first-year courses · *See* Introductory
   sequence

G

Guide to the Project Management Body of Knowledge · 12
Guide to the Software Engineering Body of Knowledge · 11

I

IEEE-CS · 1. *See* Computer Society of the IEEE
Educational Activities Board · 3
IEEE-CS/ACM Joint Steering Committee · 11
Information Systems · 2, 12
information technology · 2
Introductory Computing Sequence · *See* **Introductory sequence**.
introductory sequence
mathematics · 53
IS · *See* Information Systems
IS 2002 · 2, 78. *See* Information Systems
IS'97 · See Model Curriculum and Guidelines for Undergraduate Degree Programs in Information Systems

J

joint-curriculum task force · *See* Curriculum Task Force

L

long-life learning · 41

M

mathematical and engineering fundamentals · 23
mathematical rigor · 43
Model Curriculum and Guidelines for Undergraduate Degree Programs in Information Systems · 12
modeling and analysis · 25

N

National Association of Colleges and Employers · 9, 80
NSF · 2, 80

P

Pedagogy volunteers · 123
personal skills · 40
PMBOK · See Guide to the Project Management Body of Knowledge
problem solving · 41
Professional Practice · 24

S

SE2004 · 1
SEEK · *See* Software Engineering Education Knowledge
contact hours · 19
core · 18
determining the · 17
external reviewers · 121
internal reviewers · 121
knowledge area · 17
Knowledge Area · 21
Knowledge Unit · *See*
knowledge units · 18
levels · 17
topics · 18
unit of time · 19
Workshop · 17, 120
software
problems · 5
products · 5
software design · 27
software engienering
Code of Ethics · 10
software engineering · 5
discipline · 5
maturity · 38
vs. traditional engineering · 7
Software engineering
engineering design · 8
students · 71
Software Engineering

and computing · 6
courses · 47
definition · 6
domain-specific · 8
engineering methodology · 7
ethics · 44
evolution · 13
faculty · 71
foundations · 13
principles · 41
professional practice · 14. *See*
Professionals · 9
recurring themes · 37
undergraduate programs · 11
Software Engineering 2004 · 2
Software Engineering Coordinating
Committee · 11
Software Engineering Education Knowledge
· 1, 17
Education Knowledge Area · 2, 119
knowledge area · 20
knowledge areas · 2, 19, 37, 38
Pedagogy Focus group · 2, 3
volunteers · 2
Software Engineering Education Project ·
See
software evolution · 29
software life cycle · 32
software maintenance · *See* Software
evolution
software management · 32
software process · 30
software quality · 31
software verification and validation · 28

Software Engineering
engineering discipline · 7
Steering Committee · ii, iii, 2, 3
students · *See* Software engineering:students
Summit on Software Engineering Education
· 2, 3, 82, 125, 126
SWEBOK · 11, 12, 19. *See* Guide to the
Software Engineering Body of
Knowledge
SWECC · *See* Software Engineering
Coordinating Committee
SWEEP · *See* Software Engineering
Education Project

T

task force · *See* Curriculum Task Force
teaching technology · 45
the *Code* · *See* Code of Ethics

V

volunteer groups · 17

W

WGSEET · 3, 11, 12. *See* Working Group
on Software Engineering Education and
Training
Working Group · *See* WGSEET
Working Group on Software Engineering
Education and Training · 3, 11

Notes